The Official
Cookbook

The Official
Cookbook

By Professor Utonium

INSIGHT
EDITIONS

SAN RAFAEL · LOS ANGELES · LONDON

Contents

Introduction

To my dearest daughters, Blossom, Bubbles, and Buttercup:

Nothing brings me more joy than being your father. From the moment I created you in my lab, I have watched you grow into three smart, brave, and kind girls. With your savvy superhero skills, you keep Townsville safe every day.

But I fear I have failed you, girls. For though I have taught you how to capture criminals, roust ruffians, and vanquish villains, I have never once given you a cooking lesson! Yes, you can wrangle with wrongdoers, but can you scramble an egg? You cannot, and that is my fault.

Never fear, girls! To right this wrong, I am writing this cookbook. I am including all of your favorite recipes, as well as some new recipes for tasty treats that I have developed to keep you healthy and strong. I have also asked some of our friends to share their favorite recipes with me, and they were all very happy to contribute. (You know how much the Mayor loves his cherry pie!)

I must admit that I turned to some of our more nefarious neighbors for recipes, too. After all, bad guys can be good cooks. I learned that even a villain as sinister and utterly vile as HIM can make a darned delicious party dip. Who knew?

Before you dive into these recipes, here's an important tip: Be sure not to mix up the Chemical X with your salt shaker!

Your proud father,

Professor Utonium

Power-Up Breakfast and Brunch

Breakfast: It's the most important meal of the day. It can also be the most challenging meal of the day. Most mornings, you girls are rushing to get to school on time or zooming off to answer a call from the Mayor. That means your first sustenance intake of the morning needs to be easy to make and tasty to eat, as well as loaded with nutrition.

I have spent hours in my lab perfecting these breakfast recipes for you. There's toast loaded with healthy fiber and fats. Flapjacks with a secret protein punch. Colorful smoothies bursting with vitamins and minerals.

Some Townsville residents have chimed in with their breakfast recipes, too. Officer Mike Brikowski insisted I include a doughnut recipe. I agreed because, well, doughnuts are darned delicious.

And ultimately, it's not important exactly what you eat for breakfast, as long as you *eat* your breakfast. Don't skip it!

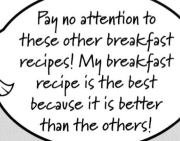

Pay no attention to these other breakfast recipes! My breakfast recipe is the best because it is better than the others!

Protein Power Pancakes

Though I love to cook pancakes for you girls, I know that you need an extra boost of energy in the morning. That's why I developed this recipe for super nutritious pancakes, packed with protein and healthy flaxseed to keep you in top form. Oh, and maximum deliciousness, too!

1 cup whole wheat flour	1 cup whole milk ricotta cheese (see tip)
1/2 cup all-purpose flour	2/3 cup milk
2 tablespoons granulated sugar	2 large eggs
1 small lemon, juiced and zested	1/2 teaspoon vanilla extract
1 teaspoon baking powder	3 tablespoons butter for griddle, plus more for serving
1/2 teaspoon baking soda	Maple syrup, for serving
1/4 teaspoon salt	

1. In a large bowl, whisk together the whole wheat flour, all-purpose flour, sugar, lemon zest, baking powder, baking soda, and salt. Make a well in the center.

2. In another medium bowl, whisk together the ricotta, milk, eggs, lemon juice, and vanilla. Pour the ricotta mixture into the well in the flour mixture; gently stir just until combined.

3. Melt a little bit of the butter on the griddle or heavy skillet over medium heat. Pour about 1/3 cup batter onto the hot griddle, spreading batter if necessary. Cook the pancakes until the bottoms are golden brown and the surface has a few bubbles, 3 to 4 minutes. Turn and cook until the bottoms are golden, 2 to 3 minutes more. Repeat with the remaining batter, adding butter as necessary.

4. Serve the warm pancakes with butter and maple syrup.

Tip: If the ricotta has a lot of liquid, drain the excess liquid in a fine-mesh strainer for 30 minutes.

Browned food tastes delicious due to the Maillard reaction. That happens when the amino acids and sugars in heated food give off melanoidins, which make food extra yummy.

Monster Avocado Toast

When some people hear the words *avocado toast*, they think of hepcats playing bongos and wearing black turtlenecks. Avocadoes may be trendy, but that's probably because they're extremely nutritious and make an excellent breakfast.

Getting you girls to eat toast piled with green goop was no easy task. Calling it Monster Avocado Toast solved the problem. Remember that giant green monster that once attacked Townsville? That beast sizzled like toast in a tangle of electrical wires. Just like a giant avocado!

You'll like making this recipe, girls. Mashing avocadoes is almost as fun as mashing monsters!

2 large ripe avocadoes, halved lengthwise, peeled and pitted

2 tablespoons fresh lime juice

Pinch salt

1 tablespoon extra-virgin olive oil, plus more for drizzling

4 eggs

4 slices whole-grain, multigrain, or sourdough bread

TOPPINGS

Everything bagel seasoning or crushed red pepper, for topping

Flaky salt (omit if using everything bagel seasoning)

$\frac{1}{2}$ cup microgreens

1. Use a large spoon to scoop the avocado flesh into a bowl. Add the lime juice and salt, then mash with a fork until fairly smooth.

2. In a large skillet, heat 1 tablespoon olive oil over medium-high heat. Fry the eggs to your desired doneness.

3. Toast the bread. Spread the mashed avocado on the toasted bread slices. Top each toast with a fried egg. Drizzle with olive oil, then top with everything bagel seasoning or crushed red pepper. Sprinkle with flaky salt if using crushed red pepper. Top with microgreens.

Let's mash some monsters!

Bubbles's Microwave Soufflés

Girls, I remember one of the first things you ever tried to cook: a cheese soufflé, for your new friend Robin Snyder. It was one of your first attempts at cooking, and it didn't come out great. But Robin is so nice that she ate it anyway with a smile on her face.

I was touched by this show of friendship. For this book, I've fixed your recipe. The result is cheesy and fluffy and a nice thing to make when friends come over for breakfast. Or any time of day!

1 tablespoon butter, softened

3 tablespoons granulated sugar, divided

3 large eggs, whites separated

⅓ cup whole milk

2 tablespoons all-purpose flour

1 tablespoon orange zest

Pure maple syrup, for serving

1 mandarin orange, peeled and separated into segments, for serving

SPECIAL EQUIPMENT

Four 6-ounce microwaveable ramekins or small coffee cups

1. Use the softened butter to grease the insides of the ramekins or coffee cups. Sprinkle the butter with 1 tablespoon sugar. Set aside.

2. Place the egg whites in a clean, ungreased large mixing bowl. Beat with an electric hand mixer until soft peaks form. Gradually add the remaining 2 tablespoons sugar. Beat until stiff peaks form. Set aside.

3. In another medium bowl, combine the egg yolks, milk, and flour. Beat with the electric mixer until smooth. Stir in the orange zest. Gradually fold the egg yolk mixture into the egg white mixture. Do not overmix. Spoon or pour into the prepared ramekins or cups. Place all the ramekins in the microwave. Microwave on high for 2 to 3 minutes or just until the soufflés stop puffing.

4. Serve immediately with a drizzle of syrup and a few pieces of orange.

When you feed your friends, it lets them know you love them!

YIELD: 4 servings

V, GF

Spicy-Hot Savory Oatmeal

Imagine my surprise when a bowl of oatmeal led to the discovery of a new power for Blossom!

Blossom, you were trying to blow on your oatmeal to cool it down when your breath turned to ice. At the urging of Bubbles and Buttercup, you transformed the kitchen floor into an ice rink. I can still feel the bump on my noggin from the slippery tumble I took that day!

That's when I realized oatmeal served too hot can burn your tongue. But oatmeal served with a touch of spiciness sure can warm up your belly on a cold morning. And that's much nicer!

4 cups chicken broth

2 cups rolled oats

¼ cup shredded Parmesan cheese

2 tablespoons olive oil

3 medium shallots, thinly sliced

1 tablespoon white vinegar or apple cider vinegar

4 large eggs

Chile oil, for topping

2 scallions, green portions only, finely chopped, for topping

1. In a small saucepan, bring the broth to a boil over medium heat. Add the oats; stir and reduce the heat to low. Cook, stirring occasionally, until the oats are tender and have absorbed most of the broth, about 5 minutes. Remove from the heat; let stand, covered, for 2 minutes. Stir in the cheese. Cover.

2. Meanwhile, in a medium skillet, heat the olive oil over medium heat. Add the shallots and cook, stirring frequently, until golden brown and crispy, 5 to 8 minutes. (Reduce the heat if the shallots begin to brown too quickly.)

3. In a large skillet, add water until the skillet is half full. Add the vinegar; bring to a boil, then reduce the heat to a simmer. Break one egg into a small dish. Holding the dish close to the water, carefully slide the egg all at once into the simmering water, taking care to not break the yolk. Repeat with the remaining three eggs, spacing them equally in the skillet. Simmer, uncovered, until the whites are completely set and the yolks begin to thicken, 3 to 5 minutes.

4. Stir the oatmeal; divide among four bowls and sprinkle with the crispy shallots. Top with a poached egg, drizzle with chile oil, and sprinkle with scallions.

Mojo-in-the-Hole

It is I, Mojo Jojo, here with a recipe for you! This is an important recipe because it is very important! Let me tell you the story of how I, Mojo Jojo, created this recipe.

One morning, I looked in my refrigerator and there was only one egg left. One egg! Everyone knows that for a nutritious breakfast, two eggs are the minimum requirement, and I had but one! I had one egg, which is just shy of two, and it was two that I needed! I immediately purchased more eggs for my breakfast.

Thus, this recipe is the perfect breakfast recipe. It requires two eggs, which creates an excellent and nutritious breakfast.

Butter or nonstick cooking spray (optional)

One 16.3-ounce container refrigerated biscuits (8 biscuits)

1 tablespoon cream or milk

½ cup finely shredded cheddar cheese

8 thin round slices deli ham

8 medium eggs

Freshly ground black pepper

1 tablespoon chopped chives or parsley (optional)

Red hot sauce, for topping (optional)

SPECIAL EQUIPMENT

2-inch round cookie cutter

1. Preheat the oven to 375°F. Grease a baking sheet or line with parchment paper. Separate the refrigerated biscuits. Lightly press each biscuit with the palm of your hand or roll with a rolling pin to flatten the biscuits to 3 inches in diameter. Place on the baking sheet. Use a 2-inch round cutter to cut out the center of each biscuit. Place the cutouts on the baking sheet next to the biscuits. Brush the top of each biscuit and cutout with the cream. Sprinkle with about half of the cheese.

2. Bake the biscuits for 10 to 15 minutes or until nearly done but not browned. Remove from the oven. Place a slice of ham on each biscuit, pressing the ham into the holes to make space (a bowl) for the eggs. Crack one egg into the center of each ham bowl. Top each egg with some ground pepper and the remaining cheese. Return to the oven for another 10 to 12 minutes or until the eggs reach your desired doneness.

3. Place two biscuits and two baked cutouts on each of four plates. Top with chives and hot sauce, if desired.

Two eggs are required!

17

Bagel Boy Breakfast Sandwich

The beauty of a bagel is that you can put almost anything you like between the two halves—and it's filled with carbohydrates to give you energy to start your day. When I order a bagel from Bagel Boy in downtown Townsville, I add protein in the form of eggs, turkey sausage, and cheese. It's yummy any way you slice it, and, fortunately, anyone can create this Bagel Boy special at home.

TURKEY SAUSAGE

1 pound 93% lean ground turkey

2 tablespoons pure maple syrup

2 teaspoons ground sage

1 teaspoon dried thyme

1 teaspoon dried oregano, crushed

1 teaspoon kosher salt

1 teaspoon coarse black pepper

1 teaspoon crushed red pepper (optional)

1 tablespoon olive oil

OMELET

8 large eggs

3 tablespoons water

2 tablespoons chopped chives

1/8 teaspoon salt

1/8 teaspoon ground black pepper

4 teaspoons butter, divided

2 tablespoons sun-dried tomato spread

4 slices mild cheddar cheese

4 everything bagels, sliced horizontally and lightly buttered

1. **To make the turkey sausage:** In a large bowl, gently combine the turkey, maple syrup, sage, thyme, oregano, salt, black pepper, and crushed red pepper, if using. Shape the turkey mixture into four patties about 1/2 inch thick.

2. In a large nonstick skillet, heat the olive oil over medium heat. Add the patties and cook until golden brown and cooked through (165°F), about 5 minutes per side. Cover and keep warm.

3. **To make the omelets:** In a medium bowl, whisk together the eggs, water, chives, salt, and black pepper. In a large nonstick skillet, melt 2 teaspoons of the butter over medium heat. Add half of the egg mixture. Cook, gently stirring and pushing the cooked portion toward the center with a spatula and allowing the uncooked egg to flow underneath, until the eggs are set and have formed an even layer in the skillet, 30 to 60 seconds.

4. Spoon 1 tablespoon of the sun-dried tomato spread over the omelets. Fold the sides of the eggs over the middle to make a rectangular shape. Slide the omelets onto a cutting board and cut in half. Top each half with a slice of cheese. Repeat with the remaining egg mixture, butter, spread, and cheese. Cover and keep warm.

5. Toast the bagels. Place a turkey patty on each bagel bottom; top with a cheesy omelet square. Add a bagel top. Repeat with the remaining bagels.

Brikowski's Favorite Glazed

Let me tell ya something, dese healthy breakfast recipes are for da birds! All you need for a breakfast is a doughnut or two. Or three. Preferably glazed. And best with a steaming hot cuppa coffee.

I like to get mine from da nearest doughnut shop. But here's a recipe for da best kinda doughnut—glazed—in case you lousy Powerpuff Girls wanna make yer own.

DOUGHNUTS

1½ cups whole milk

⅓ cup vegetable shortening

Two ¼-ounce packages instant yeast (4½ teaspoons)

⅓ cup warm water (105°F to 110°F)

2 large eggs, beaten

¼ cup granulated sugar

1½ teaspoons salt

½ teaspoon ground nutmeg

4 cups all-purpose flour, plus more for the work surface

32 to 64 ounces peanut or vegetable oil, for frying

Butter or nonstick cooking spray

SWEET VANILLA GLAZE

2 cups sifted powdered sugar, plus more as needed

3 tablespoons whole milk

1 tablespoon corn syrup or honey

2 teaspoons vanilla bean paste or vanilla extract

Pink, green, or blue food coloring, for decorating (optional)

SPECIAL EQUIPMENT

Doughnut cutter or 4-inch round cookie cutter and 1-inch round cookie cutter

Kitchen thermometer

1. **To make the doughnuts:** In a medium saucepan, heat the milk and shortening just enough to melt the shortening. Let cool until lukewarm, 105°F to 110°F. Meanwhile, in the bowl of a stand mixer or a large mixing bowl if using a hand mixer, combine the yeast and warm water. Let stand for 5 minutes to dissolve the yeast. To the mixing bowl, add the cooled milk mixture, the eggs, sugar, salt, nutmeg, and 2 cups flour. With the paddle attachment, beat on low speed until combined. Scrape the edges of the bowl and beat on medium speed for 1 minute. Gradually beat in enough of the remaining flour until the dough begins to form a ball.

2. Remove the dough from the mixing bowl onto a lightly floured surface. Lightly knead the dough with your hands until smooth and elastic, working in only enough flour to make a soft dough that is not sticky. Place in a greased bowl; cover and let rise in a warm place until doubled in size (1 to 2 hours) or refrigerate overnight.

3. If chilled overnight, let the dough sit at room temperature for 30 to 60 minutes before shaping. Line a baking sheet with parchment paper and dust lightly with flour. On a lightly floured surface, roll or pat out the dough to ¾-inch thickness. Use a doughnut cutter (or two round cutters) to cut out 4-inch doughnuts with a 1-inch hole in the center. Place the doughnuts and

the hole cutouts on the prepared baking sheet. You can reroll the dough scraps to get more doughnuts. Cover the doughnuts with a clean towel and let rise for 30 minutes.

4. Meanwhile, preheat 3 to 4 inches of frying oil in a large pan or Dutch oven to 365°F. While the oil is heating up, prepare the sweet vanilla glaze.

5. **To make the sweet vanilla glaze:** In a medium mixing bowl, whisk together the powdered sugar, milk, corn syrup, and vanilla bean paste. Whisk in extra powdered sugar as needed to make a thick glaze that pours thickly from a spoon. If desired, stir in a little food coloring in your favorite Powerpuff Girl color! Set aside.

6. Line a second baking sheet with a wire rack. When the oil reaches temperature, carefully lower three or four doughnut pieces into the hot oil with a metal slotted spoon or a spider frying utensil. Fry for about 1 minute on each side, turning them with the metal spoon. When done and nicely brown, remove the doughnuts to the second baking sheet. Repeat with the remaining dough. While the doughnuts are still warm, spoon some sweet vanilla glaze over the top of each doughnut. Serve the doughnuts warm or cooled, with coffee, of course!

Super Energy Smoothies

What is the best breakfast for three girls always on the go? Why smoothies, of course! You can whip one up in a jiffy and take it with you.

These smoothies contain colorful ingredients that are packed with nutrition. I came up with a special recipe for each of you. Blossom, strawberries and raspberries make your smoothie pink. Bubbles, your smoothie contains blueberries, of course. And Buttercup, the secret to your green smoothie is leafy greens loaded with vitamins and minerals.

BLOSSOM'S MIGHTY MIXED-BERRY SMOOTHIE

1 cup frozen strawberries

½ cup frozen raspberries

1 cup dairy, almond, or oat milk

One 6-ounce container strawberry or raspberry Greek yogurt

1 scoop vanilla protein powder

BUBBLE'S BLUEBERRY BONANZA SMOOTHIE

1½ cups frozen blueberries

1½ cups dairy, almond, or oat milk

½ cup frozen banana slices

2 tablespoons almond butter

1 scoop vanilla protein powder

1 tablespoon fresh lemon juice

1 teaspoon ground cinnamon

BUTTERCUP'S GREEN MACHINE SMOOTHIE

1 cup packed fresh spinach

½ cup sliced cucumber

½ cup frozen banana slices

⅓ cup frozen pineapple tidbits

½ cup unsweetened plant milk

1 scoop unflavored protein powder (optional)

2 tablespoons Greek yogurt

1. **To make Blossom's mighty mixed-berry smoothie:** In a high-speed blender, combine the strawberries, raspberries, milk, yogurt, and protein powder. Cover and blend until smooth. Pour into a chilled glass.

2. **To make Bubble's blueberry bonanza smoothie:** In a high-speed blender, combine the blueberries, milk, banana, almond butter, protein powder, lemon juice, and cinnamon. Cover and blend until smooth. Pour into a chilled glass.

3. **To make Buttercup's green machine smoothie:** In a high-speed blender, combine the spinach, cucumber, banana, pineapple, milk, protein powder, if using, and yogurt. Cover and blend until smooth. Pour into a chilled glass.

Note: This recipe is vegan if using a dairy-free milk option.

The Mayor's Brioche Toast with Sweet Cherry Jam

Being the Mayor of Townsville can be awfully stressful, but usually I sleep like a baby. Lately, though, I've been up at night with the strangest dream. I dream that I *am* a baby—a giant baby with luxurious hair who wails and cries because I want toast! Toast, toast, toast!

When I wake up, I beg my wife to make this breakfast for me. It's the yummiest toast I've ever had, and I top it with cherry jam because cherries are positively scrumptious.

SWEET CHERRY JAM

1½ to 2 pounds (2 cups) ripe sweet cherries, pitted and coarsely chopped, or frozen sweet cherries, thawed and chopped

4¼ cups granulated sugar

1 teaspoon almond extract (optional)

¾ cup water

One 1.75-ounce box powdered fruit pectin

2 tablespoons lemon juice

BRIOCHE

1 tablespoon active dry yeast

¼ cup warm water (105°F to 115°F)

3 cups all-purpose flour, plus more for the work surface

¼ cup granulated sugar

1¼ teaspoons salt

½ cup butter, softened

½ cup milk

4 eggs, divided

Butter or nonstick cooking spray

1. **To make the sweet cherry jam:** Prepare and clean the containers for 5 cups of jam; set aside. Place the prepared cherries in a large microwave-safe bowl. Stir in the sugar. Let stand for 10 minutes, stirring occasionally. Place in the microwave and cook on high for 3 minutes. Stir to dissolve the sugar. Microwave for 1 to 2 minutes more or until all the sugar is dissolved. Stir in the almond extract, if using.

2. Combine the water and pectin in a small saucepan, stirring to dissolve. Cook and stir over medium-high heat, bringing to a boil. Boil for 1 minute, stirring constantly. Remove from the heat and add to the cherry mixture. Stir in the lemon juice and continue stirring for 3 minutes.

MAYOR WANTS TOAST!

3. Fill the clean containers to within ½ inch of the tops. Wipe off the top edges of the containers and cover with lids. Let stand at room temperature for 24 hours. Then the jam is ready to serve. Refrigerate the jam for up to 3 weeks or freeze for up to 1 year.

4. **To make the brioche:** In a small bowl, dissolve the yeast in the warm water. Let stand for 5 to 10 minutes or until bubbly. In the bowl of a stand mixer or a large mixing bowl if using a hand mixer, combine 1 cup of the flour, the sugar, and salt. Add the butter, milk, 3 eggs, and softened yeast to the bowl. Beat until well combined. Using a wooden spoon, stir in most of the remaining flour. Turn out the dough onto a floured surface. Knead in just enough of the remaining flour to make a soft, smooth dough. Avoid adding too much flour. The dough should be very soft but not sticky. Shape it into a ball and place in a greased bowl. Cover and refrigerate for several hours or overnight.

5. Grease two 8-by-4-inch loaf pans and remove the dough from the refrigerator. On a lightly floured surface, divide the dough into six equal pieces. Roll each piece into an 8-inch rope. To make braided loaves, braid three ropes together. Pinch the ends and tuck them under. Place one braid in a prepared pan. Repeat with the remaining three ropes. Beat the remaining egg with a fork and brush onto the tops of each loaf. Cover and keep any remaining beaten egg. Cover the loaves and let rise in a warm place until doubled in size, about 2 hours.

6. Preheat the oven to 350°F. Brush the loaves again with the remaining beaten egg. Bake for 30 to 35 minutes, covering with foil for the last 15 to 20 minutes to prevent overbrowning. Let the loaves cool for 5 to 10 minutes before removing from the pans. Cool completely before slicing and toasting. Serve with sweet cherry jam.

Note: Prepare Sweet Cherry Jam at least 1 day ahead. Prepare brioche dough the day before serving.

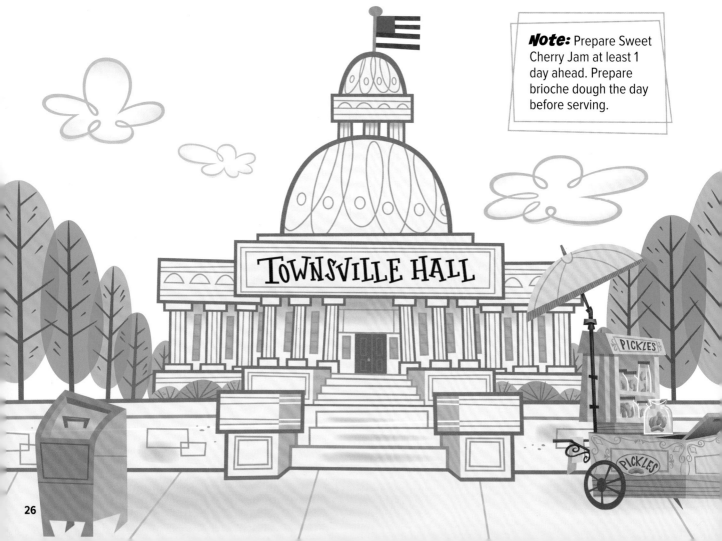

2

Awesome Appetizers and After-School Snacks

Nothing wipes away the late-afternoon blahs like a tasty snack. Sure, a handful of popcorn or a bag of chips can do the trick, but sometimes you just need something more satisfying. I've invented some appetizers and snacks based on a few of our favorite memories.

But I must warn you—word seems to have gotten around Townsville that I am writing this cookbook for you. More and more villains have been sliding their recipes under my door or hacking into my recipe files to add their own. Intrigued, I tested all of these villainous recipes in my lab, and they were quite good. As a result, I have decided to continue to include recipes from nefarious felons, for the sake of culinary excellence.

Enjoy your snacks and appetizers—but be sure not to spoil your dinner, girls!

Nefarious? Me? Why, thank you!

The Mayor's Favorite Fried Pickles

By golly, I love pickles! I love pickle dip, pickle soup, pickle-flavored potato chips, pickle casserole, pickle puttanesca . . . you get the picture. And one of my very favorite ways to eat pickles is fried and dunked in dip. Oh my, that sounds good. I need pickles right now!

RANCH DRESSING

1 cup mayonnaise

½ cup buttermilk

1 clove garlic, minced

½ teaspoon onion powder

¼ teaspoon ground black pepper

1 tablespoon finely chopped fresh dill or 1 teaspoon dried dill

1 tablespoon finely chopped chives

2 teaspoons fresh lemon juice

FRIED PICKLES

1 quart vegetable oil

12 dill pickle spears

1 cup all-purpose flour

1 teaspoon onion powder

1 teaspoon garlic powder

1 teaspoon Hungarian paprika

3 large eggs

2 cups panko breadcrumbs

SPECIAL EQUIPMENT

Kitchen thermometer

1. **To make the ranch dressing:** In a medium bowl, whisk together the mayonnaise, buttermilk, garlic, onion powder, pepper, dill, chives, and lemon juice until smooth. Cover with plastic wrap and chill for 1 hour.

2. **To make the fried pickles:** In a deep cast-iron skillet, heat the oil to 375°F. Meanwhile, lightly pat the pickles dry with paper towels.

3. In a shallow dish, stir together the flour, onion powder, garlic powder, and paprika. In a second shallow dish, whisk the eggs. Place the panko breadcrumbs in a third shallow dish.

4. Line a plate with paper towels. For each fried pickle, roll a spear in the flour mixture, then the beaten egg, back to the flour mixture, and then the egg again. Roll in the breadcrumbs. Use tongs to carefully slide the spears, one at a time, into the hot oil. Fry until golden brown, turning once, 2 to 3 minutes total. Transfer to the prepared plate.

5. Serve hot with the ranch dressing.

POWERPUFF GIRLS, IT'S AN EMERGENCY! I CAN'T GET THE LID OFF MY PICKLE JAR!

Sedusa's Date-Night Turnovers

Girls, I'd like to apologize for deceiving your father into believing I was Ima Goodlady, a kind woman who truly cared for you girls—just so I could ground you and rob the Mayor's jewels.

Just kidding! You little brats don't *really* believe a villain can turn over a new leaf, do you? I'm sure you'll never forget me, Sedusa, but just to make sure you don't, here is my *turnover* recipe. It's stuffed with savory flavors guaranteed to make your date's mouth water: bacon, goat cheese, and pecans.

1 sheet frozen puff pastry (half of a 17.25-ounce package)

6 slices thick-cut bacon, diced

½ cup diced yellow onion

One 4-ounce package goat cheese, room temperature

10 pitted dates, finely chopped

3 tablespoons finely chopped pecans, toasted

2 tablespoons finely chopped chives

1 large egg, lightly beaten

1 tablespoon water

All-purpose flour, for dusting

1. Preheat the oven to 400°F. Line a large baking sheet with parchment paper. Thaw the puff pastry according to the package directions while preparing the filling. Line a plate with paper towels.

2. In a medium skillet, cook the bacon over medium heat until crisp, about 5 minutes. Use a slotted spoon to transfer the bacon to the prepared plate. Add the onion to the hot skillet and cook until tender, 3 to 4 minutes. Use a slotted spoon and add to the bacon.

3. In a medium bowl, stir together the bacon, onion, goat cheese, dates, pecans, and chives. In a small bowl, beat the egg and water.

4. On a lightly floured surface, roll out the pastry sheet to a 12-inch square; cut into nine equal squares. For each turnover, lightly brush the pastry edges with the egg mixture and place 1 tablespoon filling in the center of each square. Fold opposite corners together to form a triangle. Crimp the edges with a fork to seal. Transfer to the prepared baking sheet. Repeat with the remaining pastry and filling. Lightly brush the tops with egg mixture; prick once on top with a fork.

5. Bake for 5 minutes; reduce the heat to 375°F. Bake until puffed and golden brown, about 15 minutes. Serve warm.

Ima Goodlady's Sweet-as-Apple-Pie Turnovers

Don't listen to that mean lady, you three wonderful girls. I, Ima Goodlady, am as sweet as these turnovers filled with apple, butter, sugar, and cinnamon. Mmm. Don't they sound divine? When I made them for Professor Utonium, he said they were the yummiest things he'd ever eaten.

1 sheet frozen puff pastry (half of a 17.25-ounce package)

2 teaspoons butter

2 medium Granny Smith apples, peeled, cored, and diced

2 tablespoons packed brown sugar

1 teaspoon apple pie spice or ground cinnamon

½ teaspoon lemon zest

Pinch salt

1 large egg, lightly beaten

1 tablespoon water

¼ cup powdered sugar

1 to 2 tablespoons heavy cream

1. Preheat the oven to 400°F. Line a large baking sheet with parchment paper. Thaw the puff pastry according to the package directions while preparing the filling.

2. In a medium skillet, heat the butter over medium heat. Add the apples and cook until softened, 4 to 5 minutes. Remove from the heat. Stir in the brown sugar, apple pie spice, lemon zest, and salt. In a small bowl, beat the egg and water.

3. Roll out the pastry to a 12-inch square; cut into nine equal squares. For each turnover, lightly brush the edges with the egg mixture and place one-quarter of the apple filling in the center of each square, spreading to within ½ inch of the edge. Fold opposite corners together to form a triangle. Crimp the edges with a fork to seal. Transfer to the prepared baking sheet. Repeat with the remaining pastry and filling. Lightly brush the tops with the remaining egg mixture; prick once on top with a fork.

4. Bake for 5 minutes; reduce the heat to 375°F. Bake until puffed and golden brown, about 15 minutes. In a small bowl, stir together the powdered sugar and cream to reach your desired consistency. Drizzle the glaze over the warm turnovers.

Why, these turnovers are simply splendid!

Imposter Octi Bread

There is no villain so utterly evil, so horribly vile, as the demonic creature known as HIM. Perhaps one of the most abominable things he did was to talk to Bubbles through her beloved stuffed octopus, Octi, trying to break you girls apart.

But you girls remembered how much you love one another and banded together to defeat HIM. When you did that, my heart became as warm and melty as this stuffed pizza bread. It's shaped like Octi, so you will never forget the lesson you learned that fateful day.

BREAD

1½ cups warm water (115°F to 120°F)

1 tablespoon granulated sugar

One ¼-ounce package active dry yeast (2¼ teaspoons)

2 teaspoons salt

4 cups all-purpose flour, plus more for the work surface

Butter or nonstick cooking spray

5 to 8 round deli slices provolone cheese

½ cup mini pepperoni slices

QUICK MARINARA DIPPING SAUCE

One 8-ounce can tomato sauce

1 teaspoon crushed garlic

1 teaspoon dried Italian seasoning

1 teaspoon granulated sugar

1 teaspoon red wine vinegar

1 tablespoon olive oil

Pinch crushed red pepper (optional)

1. **To make the bread:** In a large bowl, combine the warm water, sugar, yeast, salt, and 2 cups of the flour. Stir with a wooden spoon until well mixed. Gradually stir in more of the remaining flour until the dough begins to form a ball in the center of the bowl. Turn out the dough onto a lightly floured surface. Gently knead in enough of the remaining flour to make a dough that is moderately soft and smooth. Shape the dough into a ball and place in a greased bowl. Cover with plastic wrap and let the dough rise in a warm place until doubled in size, about 1 hour.

2. Line a baking sheet with parchment paper. Place the risen dough on a lightly floured surface, flattening to deflate a bit. Gently pat or roll out with a rolling pin to a 12-inch circle. Place on the prepared baking sheet. With kitchen scissors or a sharp knife, make eight evenly spaced 3-inch-long cuts along the edge of the circle toward the center. You will have eight sections of dough with an uncut center. Shape each section of dough into a rounded leg by tucking the cut edges underneath and pinching to seal. Spray a large piece of plastic wrap with nonstick cooking spray and use to cover the shaped dough, sprayed-side down to prevent sticking. Let the dough rise until doubled in size, about 35 minutes.

3. Preheat the oven to 375°F. Bake the shaped dough for 15 to 20 minutes or until lightly browned. Remove from the oven. Arrange the sliced cheese all over the bread, cutting the cheese as needed to cover all of the bread. Return the bread to the oven for about 3 minutes or just until the cheese begins to melt. Remove from the oven. Brush with some sauce. Arrange the pepperoni slices all over the sauce. Return the bread to the oven for 1 to 2 minutes or until the pepperoni is hot. Serve warm with the quick marinara dipping sauce.

4. **To make the quick marinara dipping sauce:** In a small saucepan, combine the tomato sauce, crushed garlic, dried Italian seasoning, granulated sugar, red wine vinegar, and olive oil. Bring to a simmer over medium heat. Simmer for 5 minutes. Stir in a pinch of crushed red pepper, if using. Serve warm or at room temperature with bread for dipping.

Rowdyruff Boys' Snips and Snails and Puppy Dog Tails Snack Mix

I, Mojo Jojo, will never forget the day I planned my greatest revenge on the Powerpuff Girls and created the Rowdyruff Boys! Before I conjured up Boomer, Brick, and Butch in a prison toilet cauldron, I asked myself, "What are little boys made of?" And the answer is what everyone knows is the answer: snips and snails and puppy dog tails.

Professor Utonium would not let me include the real recipe for making the Rowdyruff Boys. So, here is the next best thing. Use cheese puff curls instead of puppy dog tails, mini pretzels instead of snails, and snip up some dried apricots. This snack mix may not be able to defeat the Powerpuff Girls. But it is very delicious!

2 cups cheese curl puffs (puppy dog tails)

2 cups oyster crackers (snails)

2 cups broken sourdough pretzel pieces

1 cup shoestring potato sticks

½ cup slivered almonds or dry-roasted peanuts

4 tablespoons butter

3 tablespoons olive oil

2 teaspoons sesame seeds

2 teaspoons poppy seeds

1½ teaspoons dried minced onion

1 teaspoon dried minced garlic

¼ teaspoon coarse salt

¼ cup grated Parmesan cheese

1. Preheat the oven to 300°F. In a large bowl, combine the cheese puff curls, oyster crackers, pretzel pieces, potato sticks, and almonds.

2. In a small saucepan, melt the butter over medium heat. Stir in the olive oil, sesame seeds, poppy seeds, minced onion, and minced garlic. Add to the bowl and toss to combine well. Add the salt and Parmesan cheese. Toss to coat.

3. Spread the mixture in a large baking pan or sheet pan. Bake for 10 to 15 minutes or until crisp, stirring every 5 minutes. Let cool before serving. Store in an airtight container at room temperature for up to 1 week.

We wanna fight!

Mopey Popo's Banana Chips

I don't know why Mojo Jojo calls me Mopey Popo. I'm not mopey. Sure, I cry a lot. I'm never happy. I am always contemplating my true destiny. And I never do anything right, no matter how hard I try.

But could somebody mopey make delicious banana chips? I don't think so. My banana chips are awesome. They taste so good that I almost want to smile when I eat them.

So, the next time you're tempted to take over the world, don't. Make banana chips instead.

4 tablespoons water

1 tablespoon fresh lemon juice

3 ripe yet firm bananas, sliced ⅛ inch thick

Butter or nonstick cooking spray

¾ teaspoon ground cinnamon or ground ginger

¾ teaspoon kosher salt

1. Preheat the oven to 250°F or an air fryer to 212°F. In a small bowl, stir together the water and lemon juice. Place the banana slices in a medium bowl; drizzle with the water mixture and gently toss to combine.

2. **To bake banana chips in the oven:** Line two large baking sheets with parchment paper; grease with butter or spray with nonstick cooking spray. Arrange the banana slices in a single layer on the parchment paper. Stir together the cinnamon and salt. Bake for 1½ to 2 hours or until crisp, turning once after 1 hour. Peel the banana slices off the parchment paper and transfer to a wire rack to cool.

3. **To bake banana chips in an air fryer:** Cut a piece of parchment paper to fit the air fryer basket and spray with nonstick cooking spray. Arrange the banana slices in a single layer on the parchment paper; sprinkle with salt. Bake for 40 minutes or until crisp, turning once after 25 minutes. Peel the banana slices off the parchment paper and transfer to a wire rack to cool. Repeat with the remaining banana slices.

4. Store, covered, in an airtight container at room temperature for up to 3 days.

YIELD: 10 servings crackers; 20 servings fruit paste

Powerpuff Cheese and Sausage Selection

Lenny Baxter here. You may remember me, the Collector, the guy with the most complete collection of Powerpuff Girls merch in the world. I've got it all! Even the Powerpuff Cheese and Sausage Selection.

If you want it, you're out of luck because it's all mine and I'm not sharing with anybody. But because I'm trying to get released on good behavior, I *will* share the recipe on the cheese and sausage box with you. You can make a charcuterie board based on the stuff in the box, invite some friends over, and try not to feel bad that you don't have a collection anywhere as awesome as mine.

CRUNCHY SEEDY CRACKERS

- 3/4 cup all-purpose flour
- 1/4 cup whole wheat pastry flour
- 2 tablespoons sesame seeds
- 1 tablespoon caraway seeds
- 1 tablespoon flaxseed
- 1 tablespoon Italian seasoning
- 1 teaspoon lemon zest
- 1 teaspoon kosher salt
- 3 tablespoons butter, melted
- 5 tablespoons water
- 2 tablespoons roasted pepitas
- 1 tablespoon roasted sunflower seeds

APPLE-HONEY FRUIT PASTE

- 1½ pounds Honeycrisp, Gala, or Fuji apples, peeled, cored, and chopped
- 1/2 cup water
- 1/2 cup honey
- 1 tablespoon lemon juice

FOR SERVING

- Honey, apple-honey fruit paste or jam, Dijon mustard, cornichons, assorted nuts, and olives
- Cheeses of choice (for example, an aged cheddar, pungent blue, and a creamy Brie)
- Meats of choice (for example, prosciutto, Italian salami, and American salami)
- Crunchy seed crackers and/or other crackers and/or sliced bread
- Fresh fruit and vegetables, such as grapes, whole radishes, carrot sticks, and mini bell peppers

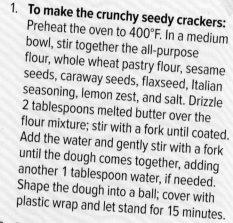

1. **To make the crunchy seedy crackers:** Preheat the oven to 400°F. In a medium bowl, stir together the all-purpose flour, whole wheat pastry flour, sesame seeds, caraway seeds, flaxseed, Italian seasoning, lemon zest, and salt. Drizzle 2 tablespoons melted butter over the flour mixture; stir with a fork until coated. Add the water and gently stir with a fork until the dough comes together, adding another 1 tablespoon water, if needed. Shape the dough into a ball; cover with plastic wrap and let stand for 15 minutes.

2. Roll out the dough between two sheets of parchment paper or waxed paper until no more than 1/8 inch thick. Remove the top piece of parchment paper; invert the dough onto a baking sheet. Remove the remaining parchment paper. Prick the dough with a fork; brush with the remaining 1 tablespoon butter. Sprinkle with pepitas and sunflower seeds; gently press into the dough.

3. Bake until light brown and crisp, 12 to 14 minutes. Transfer to a wire rack to cool. (Crackers will continue to crisp as they cool.) Break the crackers into smaller pieces. Store at room temperature in an airtight container for up to 1 week.

4. **To make the apple-honey fruit paste:** In a medium saucepan, combine the apples and water; bring to a boil over medium-high heat. Reduce the heat to medium-low. Simmer, uncovered, until the apples are tender, about 15 minutes. Drain the apples well and transfer to a blender (reserve the saucepan). Cover and purée until the apples are smooth. Transfer the apple purée to the reserved saucepan. Stir in the honey and lemon juice. Simmer, uncovered, over low heat until the mixture is thick enough for a wooden spoon to stand without falling, 45 to 60 minutes.

5. Transfer the paste to an 8-by-8-inch pan. Cool for 15 minutes. Cover and refrigerate overnight to set. Cut into squares if it's firm (fruit paste can be spreadable or firm). Store, covered, in the refrigerator for up to 2 weeks.

6. **To make the board:** Fill small ramekins with honey, apple-honey fruit paste or jam, Dijon mustard, cornichons, assorted nuts, and olives and arrange on a large cutting board or wooden tray.

7. Arrange several types of cheese on the board, allowing space for slicing and scooping. Add the meats next to the cheeses.

8. Place two or three small stacks of crunchy seedy crackers or other crackers and/or sliced bread on the board. Fill any gaps on the board with fresh fruit and vegetables. Set out the board with cheese knives, small plates, and napkins.

Bow Wow Wow Snack Mix

Girls, do you remember the time that Mojo Jojo turned everyone but you into dogs? I will confess that in my dog form, I had a strong craving for snacks. After a recent night of dreams about chasing my tail, I reached for some canine nibbles for breakfast. In my human form, they were gosh-darned awful!

I retreated to my lab, and after some experimentation, I came up with this crispy, peanut-buttery snack mix. I add extra cinnamon when I make it for you girls, and a hint of spicy cayenne pepper when I make some just for me.

1½ cups milk chocolate or semisweet chocolate chips

2 tablespoons butter

1 cup smooth peanut butter

1 teaspoon vanilla extract

1 teaspoon ground cinnamon

¼ teaspoon salt

⅛ teaspoon ground chile pepper or dash cayenne pepper (optional) (see note)

8 cups square crispy rice cereal

4 cups sifted powdered sugar

3 tablespoons rainbow nonpareils in pink, purple, and blue (optional) (see note)

1. In an extra-large microwave-safe bowl, combine the chocolate chips and butter. Microwave on high for 30 seconds. Stir and continue for another 30 seconds. Stir again. Continue until the chocolate is just melted; do not overcook. Stir the peanut butter into the warm chocolate. Stir in the vanilla, cinnamon, salt, and chile pepper, if using.

2. Add the cereal and fold with a rubber spatula or a large spoon until the cereal is evenly coated.

3. In another extra-large bowl, place the powdered sugar. Add the coated cereal to the powdered sugar, about one-quarter at a time, stirring to coat all of the cereal with powdered sugar. Add the nonpareils, if using. Keep stirring until all of the cereal pieces are coated with powdered sugar. Store in an airtight container.

Note: You can make this snack spicy for adults with the addition of hot chile pepper or you can add the colorful sprinkles for a fun party mix for kids.

HIM's Devilishly Good Dip

Helloooooo, girls! Would you like to come to a party? I've invited everyone in Townsville and nobody has accepted my gracious offer. You'd think they were afraid to hang out with the evilest of evil, the cruelest of the cruel, the King of Darkness. It's not like I'm planning on stealing everyone's souls for all eternity or anything like that. (Although if I am being honest, the thought did cross my mind.)

Sometimes even infernal majesties of evil just want to have a good time. And at the dark heart of every good party is a fabulous dip. Mix up a batch of this spicy spread and you'll have your party guests eating out of your claws.

12 hard-boiled eggs, peeled, divided

½ cup mayonnaise

4 ounces cream cheese, softened

1 tablespoon Dijon mustard

1 tablespoon finely chopped fresh chives, divided

1 teaspoon hot sauce (optional)

½ teaspoon garlic powder

Hungarian paprika, for garnish

Assorted crackers and cut-up vegetables, such as radishes, bell pepper, and carrots, for serving

1. Quarter one of the hard-boiled eggs and set aside for garnish. In a food processor, combine the remaining 11 hard-boiled eggs, the mayonnaise, cream cheese, mustard, 2 teaspoons chives, the hot sauce, if using, and garlic powder. Process until smooth.

2. Transfer to a serving bowl. Garnish with the reserved hard-boiled egg, remaining chives, and paprika. Serve with the crackers and vegetables.

Note: This recipe is gluten-free if using gluten-free crackers, or omitting the crackers.

Whip up this dip and your guests will all flip!

Nano Nuggets

When millions of Nano Bots rained down on Townsville and began to destroy our beautiful city, you girls could not fight them. Not until I used my Micro Stabilizer to shrink you all down to a molecular size. You battled those Nano Bots and saved the day once again!

Even miniature superheroes need to eat, but a full-size chicken nugget would have squashed you. These Nano Nuggets were the perfect size for your tiny tummies. Turns out this size is just right to pass around at parties, too.

TANGY DIPPING SAUCE

$\frac{1}{2}$ cup mayonnaise

$\frac{1}{4}$ cup ketchup

2 whole pepperoncini peppers, plus 1 tablespoon juice from the jar

1 teaspoon hot or mild chile powder

Dash salt

Dash pepper

CHICKEN

1 pound skinless, boneless chicken breasts

$\frac{3}{4}$ teaspoon sea salt, divided

$\frac{1}{2}$ teaspoon ground black pepper, divided

$\frac{1}{4}$ teaspoon paprika

$\frac{1}{8}$ teaspoon dried thyme

$\frac{1}{8}$ teaspoon dried oregano

$\frac{1}{8}$ teaspoon dried sage leaves

2 dashes cayenne pepper, divided (optional)

1 cup buttermilk

About 32 ounces peanut or vegetable oil, for frying

1 cup all-purpose flour

$\frac{1}{8}$ teaspoon garlic powder

SPECIAL EQUIPMENT

Kitchen thermometer

---

1. **To make the tangy dipping sauce:** In a small food processor or compact blender, combine the mayonnaise, ketchup, whole pepperoncini peppers, juice from the jar of pepperoncini peppers, chile powder, and dash each of salt and pepper. Blend until smooth. Transfer to a serving bowl. Cover and refrigerate until serving time. (Can be made up to 1 day ahead.)

2. **To make the chicken:** Cut the chicken into $\frac{1}{2}$-inch pieces. In a medium bowl, whisk together $\frac{1}{2}$ teaspoon salt, $\frac{1}{4}$ teaspoon pepper, the paprika, thyme, oregano, sage, and a dash of cayenne, if using. Add the chicken pieces and stir to evenly coat the chicken. Let stand for 10 minutes to absorb the flavor. Add the buttermilk. Stir to coat the chicken. Cover with plastic wrap and marinate in the refrigerator for several hours or overnight.

3. Line a plate with paper towels. Place the chicken pieces in a colander to drain the excess buttermilk marinade. Place the oil in a large saucepan or a 4- to 5-quart Dutch oven. Preheat the oil to 365°F. In a pie plate, combine the flour, $\frac{1}{4}$ teaspoon salt, $\frac{1}{4}$ teaspoon pepper, the garlic powder, and a dash of cayenne, if desired. Place a few pieces of drained chicken in the flour mixture, rolling around to coat the chicken. Use a slotted metal spoon to carefully place the chicken pieces in the hot oil. Fry for about 3 minutes or until golden brown. Use the slotted spoon to transfer the cooked chicken to the prepared plate. Repeat with the remaining chicken pieces. Serve with toothpicks and tangy dipping sauce.

> **Note:** For a less spicy version, omit the cayenne pepper from the chicken recipe. Use pickle juice and pickles in place of the pepperoncini peppers and juice.

Pretzel Day Pretzel Bites

I, the Mayor of Townsville, declare that every Wednesday is Pretzel Day! Have a pretzel bagel for breakfast! Slap some baloney on a pretzel roll! Top your ice cream with crushed pretzel nuggets! Or, use this recipe to whip up some warm and chewy pretzel bites in no time flat.

My, this all sounds good, doesn't it? My mouth is watering just thinking about all of those pretzels. Maybe I'm totally twisted, but I say *every* day should be Pretzel Day! Who's with me?

²/₃ cup baking soda

One 16-ounce loaf frozen white bread dough, thawed

Flour, for the work surface

One 8-ounce block sharp cheddar cheese, cut into 24 cubes

1 egg yolk

1 teaspoon water

Coarse salt

Your choice of mustard, for serving

1. Preheat the oven to 400°F. Grease a baking sheet and set aside. In a large Dutch oven or extra-large pot, bring 10 cups water and the baking soda to a boil over high heat.

2. Place the thawed dough on a lightly floured surface and cut the dough into 24 equal pieces. Place one piece of cheese in the center of each piece of dough. Pinch the edges together to seal in the cheese.

3. Use a slotted spoon to place about one-third of the balls in the boiling water. Boil for 30 seconds. Remove with the slotted spoon and place on the prepared baking sheet. Spread them apart so they do not touch one another. Repeat boiling with the remaining dough balls in batches.

4. In a small bowl, beat together the egg yolk and 1 teaspoon water. Brush the tops of the pretzel bites with the egg yolk mixture. Sprinkle with coarse salt. Bake for 10 to 12 minutes or until deep brown colored. Serve with your favorite mustard.

Tip: Thaw the bread dough in the refrigerator overnight so you are ready for Pretzel Day!

DO YOU KNOW WHY THEY CALL iT A PRETZEL? BECAUSE iT'S **KNOT** BREAD.

Mighty Mains and Superhero Sides

Supper is always my favorite meal of the day. Whether we're sitting around the kitchen table, dining in one of Townsville's unique eating establishments, or having dinner as guests at a neighbor's house, I enjoy the time with you and hearing all about your day.

I have tried to encrypt my files, but more villains got their recipes into this book. Those single-celled saps the Amoeba Boys managed to sneak in two! Even though they're chronically bad at criminal pursuits, they are surprisingly much better at the culinary arts.

These dinner recipes certainly took me on a walk down memory lane! There are meals here to celebrate Father's Day, Valentine's Day, and even a meal to celebrate the day I created you girls. But don't wait for a special occasion to make any of these recipes. Whipping up a meal for your loved ones is something you can do any day of the year.

Beef and Hog Dogs

There's nothing quite as tasty as a steaming-hot beef-and-hog dog from the Townsville hot dog cart. However, they've been shut down ever since the cart was overrun by cockroaches, thanks to the villain Roach Coach. So, when I'm craving a tube of processed meat particles at home, I make this dish, which combines the flavors of beef and pork with Italian flavors. It's almost as good as the food on the old hot dog cart (and without the roaches!).

1 tablespoon olive oil	4 all-beef hot dogs
1 medium onion, chopped	4 hoagie buns or brat buns, split
1 medium green bell pepper, chopped	4 tablespoons butter, softened
½ pound bulk Italian pork sausage (sweet or hot)	2 cloves garlic, minced
One 8-ounce can tomato sauce	1 tablespoon finely chopped fresh parsley
½ teaspoon kosher salt	1 cup giardiniera (mild or hot)
¼ teaspoon black pepper	8 slices provolone cheese

1. In a large skillet, heat the olive oil over medium heat. Add the onion and bell pepper and cook until softened, 2 to 3 minutes. Add the sausage. Cook, stirring occasionally, breaking up the sausage until browned and cooked through, and the onion and bell pepper are tender, 8 to 10 minutes. Stir in the tomato sauce, salt, and black pepper. Reduce the heat to low. Simmer, covered, for 10 minutes.

2. Meanwhile, line a plate with paper towels. Bring a saucepan of water to a boil over medium-high heat; add the hot dogs. Boil, uncovered, until the hot dogs have plumped on all sides, 4 to 6 minutes. Use tongs to transfer the hot dogs to the prepared plate.

3. Place an oven rack 4 to 6 inches from the heating element. Preheat the broiler. Place the hoagie buns, cut-sides up, on a large baking sheet. In a small bowl, stir together the butter, garlic, and parsley. Spread the garlic butter on the cut sides of the buns. Broil until lightly browned, 20 to 30 seconds.

4. Place each hot dog in a bun; top with some of the Italian sausage sauce and giardiniera. Top each hot dog with two slices of cheese, overlapping the slices. Broil until the cheese is melted, 1 to 2 minutes (watch carefully to make sure the cheese doesn't burn).

MMM. IT'S MADE FROM BEEF AND HOG!

Superhero Picnic Sandwiches

There's no nicer way to spend a sunny day than having a picnic in Townsville Park. My favorite thing to pack in our picnic basket is a classic hero sandwich, hearty enough to feed you three heroes. This one is stacked with almost every meat you can find at the deli counter and gets a kick from a layer of red onion and pickled peppers. We've never managed to finish a whole one, but that's usually because our picnics are interrupted by monster attacks. Let's make one for our next afternoon in the park and invite some friends to share it with us!

Four 6-inch sesame seed hoagie rolls

2 cups shredded iceberg lettuce

½ cup pickled cherry peppers, stemmed and chopped, or sliced pepperoncini peppers

⅓ cup olive oil

2 tablespoons red wine vinegar

1 tablespoon Dijon mustard

Salt

Black pepper

Dried oregano, for seasoning

8 ounces turkey or ham deli meat, thinly sliced

8 ounces salami, capocollo, or mortadella deli meat, thinly sliced

8 ounces roast beef deli meat, thinly sliced

8 ounces sliced Havarti, provolone, or Swiss cheese

½ cup thinly sliced red onion

1 medium ripe tomato, thinly sliced

1. On a work surface, split open the hoagie rolls and remove some of the center portions of the bread to partially hollow out the loaves. Place the lettuce and chopped cherry peppers over the bottom halves of each roll. In a small bowl, whisk together the oil, vinegar, and mustard. Drizzle half of the oil mixture over the lettuce. Sprinkle with a little salt, pepper, and oregano.

2. Layer the turkey, salami, roast beef, and then the cheese evenly over the lettuce layer. Divide the onion and tomato slices evenly over the cheese. Drizzle the remaining olive oil mixture over the cut side of the top half of the rolls. Sprinkle each roll with additional salt, pepper, and oregano. Place the seasoned roll halves on top of the sandwiches, pressing down slightly. Wrap each sandwich in plastic wrap. Chill for 1 to 4 hours or until serving time.

The Ministry of Pain's "Feast of Villainy"

Listen up, you little whippersnappers! I am Mastermind, and these are my comrades, Counterpart and Cohort. We are the Ministry of Pain, the most feared evildoers Townsville's ever known.

We're old guys with hard hearts, but we prefer our food to be nice and soft (on account of our dentures). That is why, when we villains celebrate our evil victories with food, we do it with mashed potatoes and mushy peas. And soft and juicy Salisbury steak. And we drown it all in mushroom gravy. Old-fashioned, you say? Ha! I dare you to eat this and say it's not delicious.

MASHED POTATOES

1½ pounds Yukon Gold or red potatoes, peeled if desired

2 tablespoons butter

½ teaspoon salt

¼ teaspoon ground black pepper

¼ cup milk or cream

2 tablespoons finely chopped chives

SALISBURY STEAK

1 pound lean ground beef

¼ cup panko breadcrumbs

3 tablespoons grated onion

2 tablespoons tomato paste

1 teaspoon Worcestershire sauce

1 teaspoon dry mustard

1 clove garlic, minced

½ teaspoon kosher salt

¼ teaspoon ground black pepper

1 tablespoon olive oil

MUSHROOM GRAVY

One 8-ounce package button mushrooms, sliced

1 tablespoon plus 2 teaspoons all-purpose flour

1 large clove garlic, minced

1 teaspoon dried thyme

½ teaspoon Worcestershire sauce

½ teaspoon dry mustard

¼ teaspoon salt

¼ teaspoon ground black pepper

2 cups beef broth

1 tablespoon dry sherry (optional)

Chopped fresh parsley, for garnish

BUTTERED PEAS

2 tablespoons butter

One 16-ounce package frozen peas

¼ teaspoon salt

¼ teaspoon black pepper

1. **To make the mashed potatoes:** In a large saucepan, cook the potatoes in lightly salted boiling water, covered, until tender, 20 to 25 minutes. Drain and return to the pot. Mash with a potato masher. Add the butter, salt, and pepper. Gradually add the milk to make the potatoes light and fluffy. Stir in the chives. Cover and keep warm until serving.

2. **To make the Salisbury steak:** Meanwhile, in a large bowl, combine the ground beef, breadcrumbs, onion, tomato paste, Worcestershire sauce, dry mustard, garlic, salt, and pepper. Form the mixture into four ½-inch-thick oval patties.

3. In a large heavy skillet, heat the olive oil over medium heat. Add the patties and cook until seared on both sides, turning once, 5 to 8 minutes (patties will not be cooked through). Transfer to a plate; cover to keep warm.

4. **To make the mushroom gravy:** In the same skillet, cook the mushrooms over medium heat, stirring frequently, until browned and tender, 5 to 8 minutes. Stir in the flour, garlic, thyme, Worcestershire sauce, dry mustard, salt, and pepper, scraping the bottom to loosen the browned bits. Slowly add the broth, stirring constantly. Add the sherry, if using. Cook until the gravy begins to thicken, 2 to 3 minutes. Return the patties to the skillet; cook until the patties are done (160°F), 5 to 7 minutes more. Sprinkle with parsley.

5. **To make the buttered peas:** In a medium skillet, melt the butter over medium heat. Add the peas and cook just until heated through, about 3 minutes. Sprinkle with salt and pepper.

6. To serve, divide the potatoes, steak, and peas among four dinner plates. Top the steaks and mashed potatoes with gravy.

Go back to Pokey Folks nursing home where you belong!

Accidental Sloppy Joes

Sometimes mistakes can lead to happy results. Like when I accidentally spilled Chemical X into my formula for perfect little girls and created you three superheroes instead.

Then there was that time that I forgot to form ground beef into patties, and instead of making hamburgers, I made Sloppy Joes. In fact, I made the best Sloppy Joes ever! I quickly wrote down the recipe so I wouldn't forget because happy accidents don't happen that often.

1 tablespoon olive oil	1 teaspoon sweet or smoked paprika
1 small yellow onion, chopped	1 teaspoon chile powder
1 small green bell pepper, chopped	1 teaspoon dry mustard
2 cloves garlic, minced	1 teaspoon kosher salt
1 pound lean ground beef	1/2 teaspoon ground black pepper
One 15-ounce can tomato sauce	4 brioche, pretzel, or hamburger buns
2 tablespoons tomato paste	4 slices mild cheddar cheese
1 tablespoon packed brown sugar	16 sliced bread-and-butter pickles or dill pickles
1 tablespoon Worcestershire sauce	

1. In a large skillet, heat the olive oil over medium heat. Add the onion, bell pepper, and garlic and cook until softened, 2 to 3 minutes. Add the ground beef. Cook, stirring frequently, until the beef is browned, 6 to 8 minutes.

2. Stir in the tomato sauce, tomato paste, brown sugar, Worcestershire sauce, paprika, chile powder, dry mustard, salt, and black pepper. Bring to a boil; reduce the heat to medium-low. Simmer, stirring occasionally, until thickened, 10 to 15 minutes.

3. Toast the buns, if desired. Divide the meat mixture among the bottom buns. Top with a slice of cheese, four pickles each, and the bun tops.

#1 Chef Shrimp and Tuna Teppanyaki

Once again, it is I, Mojo Jojo! Not only am I the number one villain in Townsville, but I am also the number one chef! I am the number one chef because no one is a better chef than I am. They are number two or number three chefs, but I am number one!

My specialty is teppanyaki, food cooked on a heated iron griddle. I made this for you girls the day I babysat you. You pretended you did not like it, but I know you were not telling the truth. Because anyone who eats my teppanyaki likes it! It is too good not to like!

If you do not have an iron griddle, you may use a regular griddle or a large skillet. Follow my instructions exactly if you want to succeed, and you will not fail. And do not forget the dipping sauce! The dipping sauce is something you must not forget!

RICE

1 cup Calrose rice or other medium-grain white rice

½ teaspoon salt

YAKINIKU SAUCE

1 tablespoon sake

2 tablespoons mirin

2 tablespoons granulated sugar

¼ cup soy sauce

½ teaspoon grated fresh ginger

1 clove garlic, minced

1 teaspoon toasted sesame oil

1 teaspoon toasted sesame seeds

TEPPANYAKI

6 shell-on jumbo shrimp

2 tablespoons neutral oil, such as grapeseed or vegetable

8 ounces fresh tuna, cut into cubes (see note)

1 small white onion, halved and cut into slivers

1 small zucchini, cut into matchsticks

1 small yellow squash, cut into matchsticks

1 medium carrot, cut into 2-inch pieces and then cut into thin slabs

6 shishito peppers or Padrón peppers, stems trimmed

4 shiitake mushrooms, thinly sliced

4 button mushrooms, thinly sliced

1. **To make the rice:** In a medium saucepan, combine the rice, 2½ cups water, and the salt. Bring to a boil over medium-high heat; reduce the heat to low. Simmer, covered, according to the package directions. Fluff with a fork before serving.

2. **To make the yakiniku sauce:** Meanwhile, in a small saucepan, combine the sake and mirin over medium heat. Add the sugar, soy sauce, ginger, garlic, and sesame oil. Whisk until the sugar is dissolved; add the sesame seeds. Remove from the heat. Cover until serving.

3. **To make the teppanyaki:** Peel and devein the shrimp; remove the tails. Slice the shrimp lengthwise. On a large griddle or in a heavy wok or large skillet, heat 1 tablespoon oil over medium-high heat. Add the shrimp and cook until seared, about 1 minute. Transfer to a plate. Add the remaining 1 tablespoon oil to the griddle; add the tuna and sear on all sides. Transfer to the plate with the shrimp.

4. Add the onion, zucchini, squash, and carrot to the griddle. Cook until crisp-tender, 3 to 4 minutes. Add the shishito peppers and shiitake mushrooms; cook until tender, 3 minutes more.

5. Return the shrimp and tuna to the griddle. Pour half of the yakiniku sauce over everything; toss until coated. Cook until the shrimp are cooked through and the tuna is rare (110°F to 115°F), 1 to 2 minutes.

6. Serve the teppanyaki with the hot cooked rice and remaining sauce.

Note: You can substitute 8 ounces chicken breast or top sirloin steak for the tuna. Cook the chicken until done (165°F) or steak to medium rare (135°F).

Anti-Gangreen Gang Field (Trip) Greens

I rue the day that you girls encountered the Gangreen Gang, a group of disrespectful delinquents, on a field trip at the Townsville Natural History Museum. They were a bad influence on you, Buttercup, when you briefly engaged in their bad-mannered behavior. That's why I invented this salad, filled with fresh and colorful greens full of vitamins that will give you an edge the next time you need to fight the Gangreen Gang. And the best thing is, it's so healthy that those greasy hooligans will never touch it!

GREEN GODDESS DRESSING

½ ripe avocado, pitted and peeled

⅓ cup lightly packed fresh parsley

¼ cup fresh lemon juice

2 tablespoons plain Greek yogurt

2 tablespoons extra-virgin olive oil

¼ cup lightly packed fresh tarragon

1 clove garlic, minced

½ teaspoon salt

⅛ teaspoon black pepper

SALAD

3 stalks asparagus, trimmed and cut into 1-inch pieces

One 5-ounce container mixed greens

1 watermelon radish, trimmed and thinly sliced

2 red radishes, trimmed and thinly sliced

1 large carrot, peeled and shaved into 1-inch ribbons

½ cup frozen peas, thawed

Chopped fresh chives, for garnish

1. **To make the green goddess dressing:** In a blender, combine the avocado, parsley, lemon juice, yogurt, oil, tarragon, garlic, salt, and pepper. Cover and blend until smooth.

2. **To make the salad:** In a small saucepan, add 2 to 3 inches of water. Prepare a medium bowl with ice water. Bring the water in the saucepan to a boil over medium-high heat; add the asparagus. Cook for 1 minute. Transfer the asparagus to the ice water.

3. On a platter, arrange the greens, asparagus, radishes, carrot, and peas. Spoon the dressing over the salad. Sprinkle with fresh chives.

Father's Day Steaks with Onion-Red Wine Gravy

I used to think that all I needed to be happy on Father's Day was a plate of liver and onions. And also a set of the rare Pro Excellence 2000 Golf Clubs.

I learned the hard way that wanting material items only leads to trouble. And also, though I may love liver and onions, others may find it yucky. So, this Father's Day, let's cook up a scrumptious steak dinner together and enjoy one another's company. Because what I need the most on Father's Day is quality time with my three girls!

STEAKS

1½ pounds top sirloin or strip steak, cut into 4 pieces

1 teaspoon salt

1 teaspoon packed brown sugar

½ teaspoon garlic powder

½ teaspoon paprika

½ teaspoon ground black pepper

¼ teaspoon onion powder

1 tablespoon olive oil

GRAVY

4 tablespoons butter

¼ cup finely chopped red onion

⅓ cup dry red wine

2 tablespoons all-purpose flour

2 cups beef stock or broth

1 teaspoon Worcestershire sauce

¼ teaspoon dry mustard

¼ teaspoon dried thyme

1. **To make the steaks:** Pat the steak dry with a paper towel. In a small bowl, combine the salt, brown sugar, garlic powder, paprika, pepper, and onion powder. Rub the seasoning on both sides of the steak.

2. In a large heavy skillet, heat the olive oil over medium-high heat until slightly smoking. Reduce the heat to medium. Add the steaks; sear until browned and crusty on both sides, turning once, 3 to 4 minutes total. Use tongs to sear the sides. Transfer to a plate and let rest (you'll finish cooking the steaks later).

3. **To make the gravy:** In the same skillet, melt the butter over medium heat. Use a spatula to scrape up any browned bits on the bottom. Add the onion and cook, stirring frequently, until softened, about 2 minutes. Add the wine; simmer until reduced by half, about 3 minutes. Sprinkle in the flour, stirring constantly for 2 minutes. Continuing to stir constantly, add the stock, Worcestershire sauce, dry mustard, and thyme. Bring to a boil; reduce the heat to medium-low and simmer 4 to 5 minutes.

4. Add the steaks back to the skillet, spooning the gravy over the top. Cook until your desired doneness, turning once, about 5 minutes for medium rare (130°F to 135°F).

Chicken Soup for the Criminally Incompetent

Y'know, everyone thinks dat we Amoeba Boys are lousy at being criminals. But when we all got colds and the cold germs mixed with our DNA, we created a virus that made everyone in Townsville miserable!

It was a pretty good plan, even though it happened by accident. We know that the antidote made youse all feel better. But for us, there ain't nothing like good ol' chicken soup to cure what ails ya.

1 tablespoon olive oil

1 tablespoon butter

1 medium yellow onion, chopped

2 medium carrots, chopped

2 ribs celery, sliced

2 cloves garlic, minced

1 teaspoon kosher salt

1/2 teaspoon black pepper

8 cups chicken stock or broth

One 12-ounce package frozen egg noodles or dried wide egg noodles

2 1/2 cups coarsely chopped cooked chicken (from a 2-pound rotisserie chicken)

2 tablespoons chopped fresh dill, plus more for garnish

2 tablespoons chopped fresh parsley, plus more for garnish

1 tablespoon fresh lemon juice

1. In a large pot, heat the oil and butter over medium-high heat. Add the onion, carrots, and celery and cook until softened, 3 to 4 minutes. Stir in the garlic, salt, and pepper. Add the stock; bring to a boil. Add the noodles. Simmer, covered, and cook according to the package directions.

2. Add the chicken, dill, parsley, and lemon juice. Cook until heated through, 2 to 3 minutes.

3. Ladle into six bowls. Sprinkle with additional dill and parsley, if desired.

Let's cook up some trouble, boys!

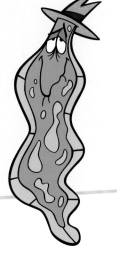

Valentine's Day Meatloaf

There is nobody I would rather spend my Valentine's Day with than you three girls. And I know how much you love my famous Valentine's Day meatloaf.

The nice thing about this meatloaf is that it's easy to put together. While it's in the oven, you can make construction-paper heart decorations for the dinner table. Before you serve it, make sure to write "Be Mine" on top with ketchup.

One more thing, girls. Can you guess what the secret ingredient of this meatloaf is?

1 cup soft breadcrumbs (see note)	1/2 teaspoon sea salt
1/3 cup milk	1/4 teaspoon black pepper
1 pound ground pork or turkey	2 large eggs, beaten
1 pound ground beef	3/4 cup grated Parmesan cheese
2 cloves garlic, minced	2 tablespoons olive oil
1/4 cup finely chopped onion	1/2 cup chile sauce
1/4 cup finely chopped pickles or pickle relish	1/2 cup ketchup
2 tablespoons finely chopped parsley, plus more for garnish	2 tablespoons brown sugar
	1/3 cup mayonnaise

1. Preheat the oven to 375°F. Line a large shallow baking pan with parchment paper. In a large bowl, soak the breadcrumbs in the milk for 5 minutes. Add the ground pork and beef, garlic, onion, pickles, parsley, salt, pepper, eggs, and cheese. Mix together with clean hands or a wooden spoon until completely combined.

2. Gather and press the meat mixture in the bowl into a ball. Transfer the ball to the prepared baking pan. Flatten the ball to a 2-inch-thick disk. Shape with your hands into a heart shape. Brush the surface of the meat with the olive oil. Bake for 30 minutes.

3. Combine the chile sauce, ketchup, and the brown sugar. Spread over the top and sides of the meatloaf. Return to the oven for 10 to 15 minutes or until an instant-read thermometer registers an internal temperature of 165°F. Let the meatloaf rest in the pan for 10 minutes before transferring to a serving plate.

4. To decorate, place the mayonnaise in a disposable pastry bag or small plastic storage bag. Snip a small opening in the tip of the bag and pipe "Be Mine" on top of the meatloaf. Garnish with extra parsley, if desired.

Note: To make soft breadcrumbs, place two or three slices of bread in a food processor. Process until coarse crumbs form. Alternatively, tear bread slices into very small pieces. Mash the breadcrumbs after the soaking step in the recipe.

Ms. Keane's Alphabet Soup

Children need tummies filled with tasty food to do their best in school. As far as I'm concerned, there's nothing better than soup. It's easy to make and filled with so many things that are good for you.

I love to add alphabet pasta to my soup. That way, you can eat and learn your ABCs at the same time. And I have an extra challenge for you girls: how many words can you make from the letters in your bowl?

1 tablespoon olive oil

1 medium yellow onion, chopped

2 medium carrots, chopped

2 ribs celery, chopped

2 cloves garlic, minced

4 cups vegetable, beef, or chicken broth

One 10-ounce bag frozen mixed vegetables, such as corn, beans, and peas

One 14-ounce can diced tomatoes

1 medium Yukon Gold potato, peeled, if desired, and chopped

2 tablespoons tomato paste

2 teaspoons Italian seasoning

1 teaspoon lemon juice

1 teaspoon kosher salt

¼ teaspoon black pepper

1 cup dried alphabet pasta

Grated Parmesan cheese, for topping

1. In a large saucepan, heat the olive oil over medium heat. Add the onion, carrots, and celery and cook until tender, 5 to 6 minutes. Add the garlic and cook for 30 seconds. Add the broth, mixed vegetables, diced tomatoes, potato, tomato paste, Italian seasoning, lemon juice, salt, and pepper.

2. Bring to a boil over medium-high heat; reduce the heat to medium-low. Simmer, covered, 5 to 7 minutes. Add the pasta; cook, covered, until the vegetables are tender, 7 to 9 minutes.

3. Divide the soup among four bowls and top with Parmesan cheese.

SOUP IS LIKE A HUG IN A BOWL!

Note: This recipe is vegetarian if prepared with vegetable broth and vegetarian Parmesan cheese.

Pizza Pie Laboratory Special

One night, I dreamed that I never created you girls by accident. Instead, you were normal, run-of-the-mill girls. Nothing exciting ever happened to us, and I had an ordinary job making pizzas in the Pizza Pie Laboratory.

Boy, was I glad to wake up from that dream! Life without accidents was so boring. The only good thing I remember from that dream was the great pizza special I made at Pizza Pie Laboratory. There is nothing average about this pie, a savory mix of meat and veggies.

DOUGH

1¾ cups bread flour or all-purpose flour, plus more for the work surface and kneading

1 teaspoon kosher salt

½ teaspoon sugar

One ¼-ounce package instant yeast (2¼ teaspoons)

1 tablespoon olive oil

¾ cup warm water (115°F to 120°F)

PERFECT LAB PIZZA SAUCE

One 6-ounce can tomato paste

½ cup crushed canned tomatoes

2 teaspoons granulated sugar

2 teaspoons dried Italian seasoning

¼ teaspoon salt

1 minced garlic clove

1 tablespoon olive oil

PIZZA

1 tablespoon olive oil, plus more for greasing the pan

All-purpose flour, for the work surface

Perfect lab pizza sauce (recipe above)

1½ cups shredded whole-milk mozzarella cheese

1 to 1½ cups your favorite meat toppings, such as cooked sausage, sliced pepperoni, Canadian bacon slices, cooked ground beef

1 to 1½ cups your favorite vegetable toppings, such as sliced mushrooms, chopped bell pepper, chopped onion

¼ cup your favorite flavor-booster toppings, such as sliced olives, sliced pepperoncini, sun-dried tomato pieces (optional)

Grated Parmesan cheese, for serving

Crushed red pepper, for serving

1. **To make the dough:** In a large mixing bowl, stir together the flour, salt, sugar, and yeast. Add the olive oil and water all at once. Stir with a wooden spoon until well combined. If needed, add more flour to make a dough that forms a ball in the center of the bowl. The dough may still be a little sticky. Turn out onto a lightly floured surface. Knead the dough a few times to make a smooth ball, using flour as needed to prevent sticking. Place the ball in a greased bowl. Cover with plastic wrap and let rise in a warm place for 1 to 2 hours or until doubled in size.

2. **To make the perfect lab pizza sauce:** In a bowl, stir together the tomato paste, crushed canned tomatoes, sugar, dried Italian seasoning, salt, garlic clove, and olive oil. Set aside.

> ***Note:*** This pizza is vegetarian if using vegetarian toppings.

3. **To make the pizza:** Preheat the oven to 400°F. Grease a 12-inch pizza pan with olive oil. Turn the risen dough out onto a lightly floured surface. With floured hands, press and stretch the dough with your fingers into a circle, about 11 inches in diameter. Transfer to the prepared pizza pan. Brush the surface of dough with 1 tablespoon olive oil. Spread the pizza sauce over the dough. Sprinkle mozzarella evenly over the sauce. Top with your meat choices, vegetables, and flavor-boosting toppings, if using.

4. Bake until the crust is browned and the cheese is bubbly, 12 to 15 minutes.

5. Let the pizza cool for 5 minutes before slicing. Serve with grated Parmesan cheese and crushed red pepper.

You don't need your own pizza laboratory to make this recipe. It's just as delicious made in your kitchen.

The Mayor's Naked Spaghetti

I'll never forget the time that Mojo Jojo gave me a good old conk on the head. When I came to, I didn't realize it, but I was in my birthday suit! I spent the whole afternoon without a stitch on.

When I went home and told the story to my wife, she laughed. And laughed. And laughed. And then she made me this dish for dinner. She calls it Naked Spaghetti. I call it gosh-darned delicious!

3 cups small cauliflower florets	3 large cloves garlic, minced
1 tablespoon olive oil	2 tablespoons finely chopped parsley, divided
½ teaspoon kosher salt	½ teaspoon crushed red pepper
½ teaspoon onion powder	½ cup freshly grated Romano cheese, divided
2 sticks unsalted butter	8 ounces dried spaghetti

1. Preheat the oven to 425°F. Line a large rimmed baking pan with foil or parchment paper. In a medium bowl, toss the cauliflower with the olive oil. Season with the salt and onion powder and toss to coat.

2. Spread in a single layer on the prepared baking pan and roast until golden and tender, stirring once, 15 to 20 minutes.

3. Meanwhile, in a small saucepan, melt the butter over low heat; stir in the garlic. Simmer, uncovered, for 20 minutes, stirring frequently (do not let the butter or garlic burn). Add 1 tablespoon parsley and the crushed red pepper; stir to combine. Stirring constantly, gradually add ¼ cup cheese.

4. While the cauliflower is roasting and the garlic butter is simmering, cook the spaghetti according to the package directions. Transfer the spaghetti to a large serving bowl. Add the roasted cauliflower to the bowl. Pour the butter-garlic sauce over everything; use tongs to toss to coat.

5. Sprinkle the remaining 1 tablespoon parsley and ¼ cup cheese over the servings.

THIS PASTA MIGHT BE NAKED, BUT YOU COULD SERVE IT AT A BLACK-TIE DINNER.

Professor's Prizewinning Chili

Girls, the last time I made this chili was for the Second Annual Townsville Chili Cookoff, which resulted in a gas monster that almost destroyed our beautiful city. That's because we each added Chemical X to the concoction, in hopes of ensuring a victory.

I regret that I didn't trust my original formula. My combination of meat, spices, onions, peppers, and a hint of coffee is a winner all on its own. Yes, the Chemical X did add something special, but I'm suggesting a pinch of cocoa powder instead.

SEASONING

2 tablespoons chile powder

1 teaspoon dried oregano

1 teaspoon kosher salt

½ teaspoon coarse black pepper

½ teaspoon ground cinnamon

Pinch ground cumin

CHILI

1 tablespoon olive oil

2 to 2½ pounds beef chuck roast, excess fat trimmed and cut into ½-inch cubes

1½ teaspoon kosher salt

½ teaspoon ground black pepper

1 cup beef stock or broth

1 medium yellow onion, diced

3 cloves garlic, minced

One 15-ounce can red kidney beans, drained

One 28-ounce can fire-roasted diced tomatoes

2 tablespoons tomato paste

1 dose Chemical X (1 chipotle pepper in adobo, finely chopped)

TOPPINGS (OPTIONAL)

Sour cream

Shredded cheddar cheese

Chopped cilantro

1. **To make the seasoning:** In a small bowl, combine the chile powder, oregano, salt, black pepper, cinnamon, and cumin. Set aside.

2. **To make the chili:** Line a plate with paper towels. In a Dutch oven or large pot, heat the oil over medium-high heat. Season the meat with the salt and black pepper. In a single layer, sear half of the meat at a time until well browned on all sides. Transfer each batch to the prepared plate. Reduce the heat to medium. Carefully drain off any fat.

3. Add ¼ cup of the stock to the Dutch oven; use a wooden spoon or spatula to scrape up browned bits from the bottom. Add the onion. Cook, stirring frequently, until softened, 3 to 4 minutes. Stir in the garlic and seasoning. Add the remaining ¾ cup stock, the beans, tomatoes, tomato paste, and chipotle.

4. Bring to a boil over medium-high heat; reduce the heat to medium-low. Simmer, covered, stirring occasionally, until the meat is tender, about 2 hours. Serve with sour cream, cheese, and/or chopped cilantro, if using.

YIELD: 6 servings
GF

Salami Swami's Antipasto Salad

Remember me, the Salami Swami? With the melodious music of my magical flute, I can charm links of salami sausages into doing my bidding.

Alas, that got me into big trouble once, when I used the salami to steal from the Townsville Museum. But I have seen the error of my ways. The best use for salami is what it was meant for: a salty staple in a delicious antipasto salad.

DRESSING

¼ cup extra-virgin olive oil

2 tablespoons balsamic vinegar

1 teaspoon Dijon mustard

1 small clove garlic, minced

½ teaspoon dried oregano

¼ teaspoon kosher salt

⅛ teaspoon black pepper

SALAD

2 hearts romaine, chopped

One 12-ounce jar roasted red bell peppers, drained, patted dry, and chopped

1 cup halved cherry tomatoes

One 6-ounce container bocconcini (miniature fresh mozzarella balls)

One 6-ounce jar marinated artichokes, drained and quartered

4 ounces salami, sliced and halved

4 ounces sliced prosciutto, cut into bite-size pieces

½ cup pitted marinated olives, halved

Small basil leaves, for garnish

1. **To make the dressing:** In a small bowl, whisk together the olive oil, vinegar, mustard, garlic, oregano, salt, and black pepper until smooth.

2. **To make the salad:** Put the romaine in a large serving bowl. Drizzle with some of the dressing; toss to lightly coat. Arrange the roasted peppers, cherry tomatoes, cheese, artichokes, salami, prosciutto, and olives in separate sections on top of the greens. Lightly drizzle with some of the dressing. Sprinkle with basil leaves.

Make salad, not crime!

Maid Mary's Happy Stew

Hi, boys and girls. It's Whimsical Willy, the sad clown. Put on your magic trousers. It's time to make a whimsical, wonderful, funderful recipe together.

Today, we're making Maid Mary's Happy Stew! You see, some things *do* make me happy, like cheeseburgers. This stew has all the ingredients of a cheeseburger simmered together in one big wondrous bowl.

4 slices thick-cut bacon, chopped

1 pound lean ground beef

1½ teaspoons kosher salt, divided

1 teaspoon black pepper, divided

1 medium yellow onion, chopped

2 ribs celery, chopped

8 tablespoons butter (4 tablespoons softened), divided

4 cloves garlic, minced, divided

¼ cup all-purpose flour

4 cups beef broth

1 cup whole milk

One 14.5-ounce can diced tomatoes, drained

One 6-ounce can tomato paste

¼ cup ketchup

1 teaspoon Worcestershire sauce

1 pound russet potatoes, peeled and diced

2 cups shredded cheddar and American cheese blend

2 tablespoons yellow mustard

6 slider hamburger buns

TOPPINGS (OPTIONAL)

Sliced pickles

Chopped onions

Ketchup

Mustard

Shredded lettuce

1. Line a plate with paper towels. In a large saucepan or pot, cook the bacon over medium heat until crisp, 8 to 10 minutes. Transfer to the prepared plate. Let cool, then crumble.

2. Line a second plate with paper towels. In a medium bowl, gently combine the ground beef, 1 teaspoon salt, and ½ teaspoon pepper. Shape into 12 small patties, about ¼ inch thick. Add the patties to the

saucepan; cook, turning once, until browned and cooked through, 4 to 5 minutes. Transfer to the prepared plate. Drain the fat from the pan.

3. Add the onion and celery to the saucepan; season with the remaining ½ teaspoon pepper and cook until tender, 3 to 4 minutes. Add 4 tablespoons of the unsoftened butter; stir in half of the minced garlic and flour. Cook, whisking constantly, until

bubbly, 2 to 3 minutes. Gradually add the broth and whisk until the flour is fully incorporated. Whisk in the milk. Add the diced tomatoes, tomato paste, ketchup, Worcestershire sauce, and potatoes. Bring to a boil over medium-high heat; reduce the heat to medium-low. Simmer, covered, until the potatoes are tender, 10 to 12 minutes.

4. Stir in the cheese until melted. Add the mustard and beef patties. Turn off the heat. Let stand, covered, for 5 minutes. Meanwhile, in a small bowl, stir together the remaining 4 tablespoons of softened butter, remaining garlic, and remaining $\frac{1}{2}$ teaspoon salt. Spread the garlic butter on the cut sides of the hamburger buns. Toast the buns lightly in a nonstick skillet over medium-low heat.

5. Serve the stew topped with crumbled bacon, hamburger buns, pickles, onions, ketchup, mustard, and/or lettuce, if using.

Eat 'Em to Beat 'Em Broccoli with Cheese Sauce

Do you remember how much you girls used to hate broccoli? I could never get you to eat those nutrient-packed sprouts, no matter how much I pleaded.

That all changed when the Broccoloids invaded Townsville. Thanks to a heaping helping of cheese sauce, you and the kids of Townsville chowed down on the Broccoloid warriors and once again saved the day!

Since then, I have figured out the secret to getting you to eat broccoli at home. Smother it in cheese sauce and add tasty toppings!

1 tablespoon olive oil	1 cup whole milk
4 medium shallots, thinly sliced	8 ounces sharp cheddar cheese, shredded (see note)
1 head broccoli, cut into florets	½ teaspoon garlic powder
2 tablespoons butter	⅛ teaspoon smoked paprika or cayenne pepper
2 tablespoons all-purpose flour	½ teaspoon salt

1. In a medium skillet, heat the olive oil over medium heat. Add the shallots and cook until golden, about 2 minutes. Set aside until serving.

2. In a large saucepan, bring a few inches of water to a boil; place a steamer basket in the pan; add the broccoli, cover, and cook until tender-crisp, 3 to 4 minutes. Drain. Cover to keep warm.

3. Meanwhile, in a medium saucepan, melt the butter over medium heat. Sprinkle the flour over the butter, whisking constantly; cook for 1 to 2 minutes (don't let it brown). Gradually whisk in the milk. Cook, whisking constantly, until the milk begins to thicken, 2 to 3 minutes. Remove from the heat.

4. Stir in half the cheese, the garlic powder, smoked paprika, and salt until smooth. Add the remaining cheese and stir until smooth. Pour some of the cheese sauce over the broccoli. Sprinkle each serving with the shallots.

5. Refrigerate leftover sauce in an airtight container for up to 3 days.

Note: For the best cheese sauce, grate your own cheese. Purchased shredded cheese contains anti-clumping agents that affect how it melts.

All-of-the-Oranges Salad

I'll never forget the day when we Amoeba Boys committed the greatest crime in the history of Townsville! The three of us multiplied . . . and multiplied . . . and multiplied. We was a regular army of criminals! And we unleashed our criminal genius on the city and stole every single orange in Townsville. We left the city without citrus, and everyone got scurvy!

What's an amoeba army to do with all of them oranges? Why not make a refreshing salad? This one is scrumptious and loaded with vitamin C.

SALAD

1 pink grapefruit
1 naval orange
1 Cara Cara orange
1 blood orange
1 tangerine

VINAIGRETTE

1 tablespoon sherry vinegar
1 teaspoon fresh lemon juice
½ teaspoon honey
¼ teaspoon Dijon mustard
¼ teaspoon kosher salt
⅛ teaspoon black pepper
¼ cup extra-virgin olive oil
Chopped fresh chives, for garnish

1. **To make the salad:** For each piece of fruit, slice off the top and bottom. Stand the fruit upright on the cutting board. Starting at the top of the fruit, guide your knife down to the base, curving the knife with the shape of the fruit. Continue all the way around the fruit until all of the rind and pith is removed. Go back and slice off any remaining pith. Turn the fruit on its side and slice into ¼-inch-thick pieces.

2. **To make the vinaigrette:** In a small bowl, whisk together the vinegar, lemon juice, honey, mustard, salt, and pepper. Gradually whisk in the oil until emulsified.

3. Arrange the citrus on a serving platter. Drizzle your desired amount of vinaigrette over the fruit. Sprinkle with chives.

Orange you glad you read this recipe?

Daring Drinks

Girls, I have an important observation: Never take a vacation from hydration! Fluids deliver nutrients to your cells and lubricate your joints, and drinking enough fluids can also improve your mind and your mood.

Water can accomplish all of these goals, but I have a theory that beverages in fun flavors with nutrient boosts can encourage children like you to meet all of their fluid needs. In short, drinks made with imagination can increase your hydration!

Oh, and villains keep delivering recipes to me in quite unusual ways. I woke up one morning to find a recipe from the Sandman tucked under my pillow!

Make mah drink already!

Chemical X-cellent

YIELD: 6 servings
V+, GF

If you were hoping for the recipe for Chemical X in this cookbook, I am sorry to disappoint you. Were that formula to get into the wrong hands, the results could be disastrous. Instead, I am sharing this recipe for a beverage with the same colorful kick as Chemical X, but without the superpowered side effects.

Nevertheless, this is no simple brew. Tart lime juice balances out the sweet watermelon juice. Fermented tea adds a dash of umami. And to mimic Chemical X, you can use hard candy gasified with carbon dioxide under superatmospheric pressure (also known as popping candy, available in your local shop in colorful packages).

4 limes, divided

Honey or corn syrup

Watermelon-flavored popping candy, for garnish

One 0.5-ounce package fresh mint, 6 leaves reserved

4 cups chopped watermelon, thawed if frozen

1/3 cup fresh lime juice

One 16-ounce bottle kombucha, such as ginger, watermelon, grapefruit, or tangerine

Apple cider vinegar, for topping

1. Juice three of the limes. Cut the remaining lime into seven wedges.

2. Wet the rim of each of six tall glasses with honey or corn syrup. Place the popping candy in a shallow dish. Dip the glass rims in the popping candy.

3. Place a mint sprig in each glass and carefully press a muddler or spoon against the mint leaves.

4. In a blender, combine the watermelon and lime juice. Cover and blend until smooth. Divide the watermelon mixture among the glasses; top with the kombucha and a splash of vinegar. Garnish each with a reserved mint leaf and lime wedge.

Fuzzy Lumpkins's "Get Offa Mah Property" Spicy Ginger-Grapefruit Punch

YIELD: 4 servings

V+, GF

Ah reckon there's nothing ah like better than some old-time relaxation. Ah hardly never get time for it, though, thanks to those durned trespassers who won't get offah mah property!

But when ah do relax, ah take a deep breath and sit in mah good ol' rockin' chair. Ah fill up mah good ol' jug with water, usually, but on them special occasions ah mix up a big ol' batch of this punch. It's a little bit sour, like me, and it's got a good fizz that makes mah fuzzy heart happy. It's durned refreshing, ah tell ya!

SIMPLE SYRUP

³/₄ cup water

³/₄ cup granulated sugar

¹/₂ cup peeled and sliced fresh gingerroot

PUNCH

16 ounces grapefruit juice

¹/₄ cup fresh lime juice

8 ounces ginger ale, divided

1. **To make the simple syrup:** In a small saucepan, stir together the water and sugar over medium heat until the sugar is dissolved. Stir in the ginger. Bring to a low boil. Reduce the heat to low. Cover and simmer for 10 minutes. Remove from the heat. Let cool and steep in a covered pan for about 1 hour. Remove the ginger with a slotted spoon.

2. **To make the punch:** In a large pitcher, combine the grapefruit juice, lime juice, and ¹/₂ cup of the simple syrup. Stir to combine. Divide the grapefruit mixture among four highball glasses; top each with about ¹/₄ cup ginger ale.

You done with yer readin' yet? Good. Now GET OFFA MAH RECIPE!

YIELD: 4 servings
V+, GF

Princess Morbucks's Fancy Water on the Rocks

You girls think you're so great because you are Powerpuff Girls and I'm not. One day, I WILL be a real Powerpuff Girl, just like you. But in the meantime, I'll enjoy being stinkin' rich. And that means all the fancy water I want!

If one of daddy's servants brings me plain water, I'll scream! I want the fancy water—no, the fanciest water! Water that's even too good for movie stars or supermodels. And it better be on the rocks, or else!

HONEYDEW-CUCUMBER-MINT WATER

1 cup honeydew chunks

1 cucumber, sliced

1 sprig fresh mint

5 cups water

BLACKBERRY-ORANGE-GINGER WATER

1 cup blackberries

1 orange, thinly sliced

One 1-inch piece fresh ginger, peeled and sliced

5 cups water

LEMON-STRAWBERRY-BASIL WATER

1 lemon, sliced

1 cup blueberries

2 sprigs rosemary

5 cups water

1. **To make the honeydew-cucumber-mint water:** In a pitcher, place the honeydew, cucumber, and mint. Add the water and chill for at least 2 hours. Add ¼ cup ice cubes to each of four rocks glasses and fill with the infused water.

2. **To make the blackberry-orange-ginger water:** In a pitcher, place the blackberries, orange, and ginger. Add the water and chill for at least 2 hours. Add ¼ cup ice cubes to each of four rocks glasses and fill with the infused water.

3. **To make the lemon-strawberry-basil water:** In a pitcher, place the lemon slices, blueberries, and rosemary. Add the water and chill for at least 2 hours. Add ¼ cup ice cubes to each of four rocks glasses and fill with the infused water.

This water is perfect, just like me!

YIELD: 4 servings
V+*, GF

"Sand-Sprinkled" Chamomile Latte

Hello there, girls, good to see you again!
Although I'm not sure if you think
   I'm a friend.
Once I built a machine that was
   oh so clever.
A machine to put the whole world
   asleep forever.

But you three girls put an end
   to my schemes.

You found me and fought me
   inside my dreams.
My machine is gone, but here's a
   recipe instead:
Drink a cup of this latte before
   you go to bed.
It's got chamomile to make you
   drowsy as can be,
To help you fall asleep, so you
   won't need me!

TEA

2 tablespoons loose-leaf chamomile
tea or 4 chamomile tea bags

4 cups water

2 tablespoons honey

1 teaspoon vanilla extract

FROTHED MILK

3 cups dairy milk, or for a vegan version
use oat milk, or almond milk

1 teaspoon ground cinnamon, for garnish

1. **To make the tea:** If using loose-leaf tea, place the tea in an infuser or filter. In a small saucepan, bring the water to a simmer over medium-high heat. Remove from the heat and add the tea; cover and steep for 6 to 8 minutes. Remove the infuser or bags. Stir in the honey and vanilla.

2. **To make the frothed milk:** While the tea is steeping, in a small saucepan, heat the milk to a simmer over low to avoid scorching, 135°F to 150°F (do not boil). To use a frother (see note), place the warm milk in a tall cup, holding it at a slight angle. Insert the frother, and froth the milk until you've reached your desired consistency, 15 to 20 seconds.

3. Pour or ladle the tea into four large cups. Pour or spoon the frothed milk on top, and sprinkle with cinnamon.

Notes: If you don't have a frother, there are several other options to make frothed milk. You can simply whisk the warm milk in the saucepan until frothy. A second option is to carefully pour the warm milk into a large French press and pump the plunger until frothy, 10 to 15 seconds. (Don't fill the French press too high as the milk will increase in volume when frothed.) A third option is to use an immersion blender—just make sure the warm milk is in a tall vessel.

Bubbles's Boffo Bubble Tea

I sure love it when chemistry collides with the culinary arts! That's what I thought the first time I tried bubble tea, and those tasty boba pearls popped in my mouth.

When I set out to invent my own bubble tea recipe, I thought of you, Bubbles, of course! Your favorite color, blue, was my inspiration. And I made it just as sweet as my most kindhearted little crime fighter.

SPICED SYRUP

1 cup granulated sugar

1 cinnamon stick

1 whole anise star (adds licorice flavor; optional)

2 whole cloves

1 teaspoon vanilla extract

TEA

One 8.8-ounce package quick-cooking dried black boba tapioca pearls

⅔ cup dried butterfly pea flower buds

2 cups boiling water

One 13.5-ounce can unsweetened coconut milk

⅔ cup sweetened condensed milk

Crushed ice, for serving

SPECIAL EQUIPMENT

Boba straws

1. **To make the spiced syrup:** In a saucepan, combine 1 cup water, the sugar, cinnamon stick, anise star, and cloves. Bring to a boil over medium-high heat, then remove from the heat and let stand for 15 minutes. Remove the spices with a spoon. Stir in the vanilla. Place the syrup in a bowl and chill in refrigerator for at least 30 minutes.

2. **To make the tea:** Bring 1 quart water to a boil in a medium saucepan over medium-high heat. Add the boba pearls; reduce the heat to medium-low and simmer for 7 minutes, stirring gently, until the pearls float to the surface and are tender. Drain the pearls in a colander. Rinse with cold water and add to the chilled syrup in the refrigerator.

3. Place the dried butterfly pea flower buds in a small bowl. Pour 2 cups boiling water over the buds. Let steep for about 10 minutes or until a deep sapphire blue color. Strain the tea through a fine-mesh sieve into a liquid measuring cup. Chill the tea while assembling the remaining ingredients.

4. In a 4-cup liquid measuring cup, whisk the coconut milk until smooth. Whisk in the sweetened condensed milk.

5. When ready to serve, divide the boba and syrup among four 12-ounce tall glasses. Pour the coconut milk mixture over the boba, about one-third up the glasses. Add enough crushed ice to fill the glasses to the top. Pour the chilled pea flower tea over the ice. Add boba straws and swirl once or twice to gently blend. Serve immediately.

The Mayor's "Singing" Apple Juice Sipper

Back when I was a young Mayor, I graced the vaudeville stage. Folks went crazy for my act. I made sweet, sweet music with my singing apple juice glasses. I was a regular virtuoso, I tell ya!

After I perfected my pitch, I moved on to improve my apple juice recipe. The result is a delightful concoction that the young people today call a mocktail. I guarantee it will make beautiful music in your mouth.

Two 1-inch pieces fresh ginger, peeled

3 oranges, zested and juiced (1 cup juice)

4 lemons, zested and juiced (1 cup juice)

5 limes, zested and juiced (½ cup juice)

1 cup chilled sparkling apple cider

Lemon or orange slices, for garnish

1. In a cocktail shaker, muddle one piece of ginger. Add ½ cup orange juice and half of the orange zest, ½ cup lemon juice and half of the lemon zest, ¼ cup lime juice and half of the lime zest, and ice to about 1 inch from the top of the shaker; shake for 30 seconds.

2. Strain into two coupe glasses. Top each glass with ¼ cup sparkling apple cider. Repeat with the remaining ginger, juices, zest, and cider. Garnish with a lemon slice.

YIELD: 6 servings
V, GF

Moejisha's Special Secret Recipe "Tea"

Hi, girls! I am Moejisha, a regular little human girl just like you regular little human girls.

Ha ha! I fooled you. I am not Moejisha. It is I, Mojo Jojo! I tricked you, just like the time you had a sleepover party and you were tricked by me. I fooled all of your silly little friends and even made you some delicious tea for your party using my great-grammy's supersecret recipe. Why is it so secret, you ask? Because it is not really tea. It is hot chocolate in disguise. Just like me, because I am in disguise, too!

4 cups whole milk

2 cups heavy cream

One 12-ounce package semisweet chocolate chips

1 teaspoon vanilla extract

½ cup creamy peanut butter

Sweetened whipped cream, for garnish

Halved mini peanut butter cups, for garnish

1. In a 3½- to 4-quart slow cooker, combine the milk, cream, and chocolate chips. Cover and cook on low for 4 hours or on high for 2 hours, whisking once halfway through. Whisk in the vanilla and peanut butter. Cover and let stand for 10 minutes.

2. Ladle into six mugs and top with whipped cream and peanut butter cups.

Dominating Desserts

Like any scientific experiment, any meal you make can fail. Your spaghetti can come out too squishy, your toast might be burnt, or your string beans might be extra stringy.

If you fail, don't despair—serve dessert! Just like you girls save the day from monsters and criminals, a sweet treat can save your meal and make everyone forget about your food failures.

Homemade desserts are always a treat, but so is ice cream from the Townsville Ice Cream Truck, or Turkish delight, taffy, or gummy shapes from the local candy shop. Working in my lab, I've reformulated these recipes so you can make them easily at home.

More villains inserted recipes into this chapter, including Princess Morbucks. She showed up at my lab and had a temper tantrum, demanding that I put her recipe in this book. I gave in just so I could resume my work in peace and quiet. I am certainly glad you girls are not spoiled little princesses!

Make my recipe or I will tell my DADDY!

Townsville Ice-Cream Truck Treats

There's nothing quite as refreshing as a treat from the Townsville Ice-Cream Truck on a hot summer day. But with all the traffic jams caused by giant monster attacks and marauding miscreants, the truck isn't always around when you're craving a good old-fashioned ice-cream sandwich.

I got to work trying to re-create this ice-cream classic in my lab, and I believe I have made it even better with fresh new flavors and colors that remind me of you girls.

CAKE LAYERS

Vegetable oil, for greasing the pans

1 cup all-purpose flour

1 cup granulated sugar

1/2 teaspoon baking soda

1/8 teaspoon salt

1/2 cup butter

3 tablespoons cocoa powder

1/2 cup water

1 egg

1/4 cup buttermilk

ICE-CREAM FILLING

2 cups vanilla ice cream, softened

1 or 2 drops blue gel food coloring

1 1/2 cups raspberry sherbet or pink strawberry ice cream

1 1/2 cups green pistachio ice cream or lime sherbet

Whipped cream and ice-cream sprinkles, for serving (optional)

1. Preheat the oven to 350°F.

2. **To make the cake layers:** Grease two 9-by-5-inch loaf pans. Line the pans with parchment paper. In a medium bowl, stir together the flour, sugar, baking soda, and salt.

3. In a small saucepan, combine the butter, cocoa powder, and water over medium heat. Bring just to a boil, stirring constantly. Remove from the heat. Add to the flour mixture. Beat with an electric hand mixer until well combined. Beat in the egg and buttermilk until well combined. Divide the batter evenly between the prepared loaf pans. Bake for 10 to 12 minutes or until a toothpick inserted in the center comes out clean. Let cool in the pans on a wire rack for 10 minutes. Use the parchment paper liners to lift the cakes from the pans. Place the cake layers in the freezer for at least 1 hour.

4. **To make the ice-cream filling:** In a medium bowl, stir together the softened vanilla ice cream and blue food coloring until well combined and no streaks are visible. Place in the freezer to firm up a bit while preparing the rest of the steps.

5. Line a 9-by-5-inch loaf pan with plastic wrap or parchment paper. Place one frozen cake layer in the bottom of one of the pans. Spread the cake layer with the blue ice cream. Return to the freezer until firm, about 1 hour. Meanwhile, let the raspberry sherbet

soften at room temperature for 20 to 30 minutes. Spread the softened sherbet over the blue ice cream. Return the pan to the freezer until firm, about 1 hour. Meanwhile, let the green pistachio ice cream soften at room temperature for 20 to 30 minutes. Spread the softened pistachio ice cream over the raspberry sherbet in the pan. Top with the remaining frozen layer of cake. Press down firmly to make full contact with the ice cream. Cover and freeze for a few hours or overnight.

6. To serve, use the plastic wrap or parchment paper liner to lift the frozen loaf from the pan. Use a warm, sharp knife to cut 1-inch slices and place on serving plates. Serve immediately or place the plates in the freezer to hold, up to an hour or so. If desired, top each serving with a dollop of whipped cream and some ice-cream sprinkles.

Le Dunne King Donnet's 5-Star Doughnuts

As you girls know, Townsville is a vibrant city filled with culinary delights! We even have a five-star restaurant: Le Dunne King Donnet. I must confess that even though dishes like their fancy foie gras with endive foam are dazzling, my favorite is their decadent doughnut dessert.

This doughnut is so good that I asked the chef for the recipe so I could make it for you at home. And it's not your basic breakfast doughnut. These fluffy cake doughnuts are filled with sparkle and shine and perfect for celebrating big moments, like saving the town from evil.

DOUGHNUTS

Vegetable shortening or nonstick cooking spray, for greasing the pans

½ cup butter, melted

¼ cup granulated sugar

¼ cup brown sugar

2 large eggs

1 teaspoon vanilla extract

2⅔ cups all-purpose flour

1½ teaspoons baking powder

¼ teaspoon baking soda

1 teaspoon ground cinnamon

½ teaspoon ground nutmeg

¾ teaspoon salt

1½ cups sparkling apple cider

1 small apple, cored and chopped (see note)

SPARKLING GLAZE

2 tablespoons melted butter

3 tablespoons sparkling apple cider

1½ cups powdered sugar

Gold coarse decorating sugar or other gold sprinkles

Gold luster dust

Edible flowers (optional)

1. **To make the doughnuts:** Preheat the oven to 375°F. Generously grease two 6-doughnut baking pans with shortening or cooking spray. In a large mixing bowl, combine the butter, granulated sugar, and brown sugar. Beat with a fork until smooth. Add the eggs and vanilla and beat until combined.

2. In a medium bowl, whisk together the flour, baking powder, baking soda, cinnamon, nutmeg, and salt. Add the flour mixture and sparkling apple cider alternately in batches to the sugar mixture, stirring to combine after each addition. Stir in the chopped apple.

5-Star Doughnuts for my three little stars!

3. Spoon the batter into the doughnut pans, filling the cavities nearly full. Bake until lightly browned and a toothpick inserted comes out clean, 12 to 15 minutes.

4. **To make the sparkling glaze:** While the doughnuts bake, in a medium mixing bowl, stir together the butter, sparkling apple cider, and powdered sugar to make a glaze that is the consistency of thick syrup. Keep covered until ready to use. (If the glaze becomes thick while standing, stir in a little more sparkling apple cider, 1 teaspoon at a time.) If desired, tint the glaze with a little golden-yellow food coloring.

5. Once the doughnuts are done baking, immediately invert the pans over a wire rack to remove the doughnuts. While still warm, spoon sparkling glaze over the tops of the doughnuts and sprinkle with gold sugar and luster dust before the glaze sets. Serve warm or cooled with a few edible flowers on top, if desired.

Note: Any apple variety will do, but it's best to avoid Red Delicious apples for this recipe.

Mr. Mime's Black-and-White Cake

What have I, Rainbow the Clown, been doing ever since the Powerpuff Girls put me in this dingy jail? (Even though it wasn't my fault when I got doused in bleach, turned into Mr. Mime, and drained all of the color and fun from Townsville. I couldn't help myself!)

Well, I'm not holding a grudge, that's for sure! Instead, I've been practicing my baking. The outside of this cake is black and white, like my old evil alter ego. But the inside is filled with beautiful colors, just like me!

CAKE

6 egg whites

Vegetable oil, for greasing the pans

3 cups all-purpose flour

1½ teaspoons baking powder

¾ teaspoon baking soda

¾ teaspoon salt

¾ cup butter, softened

3 cups granulated sugar

2 cups buttermilk

1 teaspoon vanilla extract

1 teaspoon almond extract

Pink, blue, and green food coloring, for decorating

BUTTERCREAM FROSTING

6 ounces pasteurized egg whites

24 ounces sifted powdered sugar

2 teaspoons clear vanilla extract

½ teaspoon salt

24 ounces unsalted butter, room temperature

Blue gel food coloring, for decorating

1. Let the egg whites stand at room temperature for 30 minutes. Grease and lightly flour three 8- or 9-inch round cake pans. Preheat the oven to 350°F.

2. **To make the cake:** In a large bowl, whisk together the flour, baking powder, baking soda, and salt. Set aside. In the large bowl of a stand mixer, beat the butter for 30 seconds. With the mixer on medium-high, gradually add the sugar. Scrape the sides of the bowl and beat until very fluffy, about 3 minutes. Add the egg whites, a little at a time, beating well after each addition. Alternately beat in the flour mixture and then the buttermilk, beating until combined after each addition. Beat in the vanilla and almond extracts. Scrape the bowl and beat to combine well. Divide the batter equally into three bowls. (Using a kitchen scale helps with accuracy.)

3. Stir the pink food coloring into one portion of the batter, blue into another portion, and green into the third portion. Spread the pink batter

evenly into one prepared pan. Spread the blue and green batters into the other pans, respectively. Bake until a toothpick inserted in the centers of the cakes comes out clean, 25 to 30 minutes. Cool the pans on wire racks for 10 minutes. If the tops are rounded, use a long, serrated knife to trim the tops to be level while the cakes are still in the pans. (If they're rounded but beneath the edges of the cake pans, remove the cakes from the pans, then carefully trim the tops as level as you can by just eyeballing it without the guide of the pans.) Remove the cakes from the pans. Let cool completely on the wire racks.

4. **To make the buttercream frosting:** Place the egg whites and powdered sugar in the bowl of a stand mixer or a large mixing bowl if using a hand mixer. Attach the whisk attachment and combine the egg whites and powdered sugar on low. Beat on high until the powdered sugar is dissolved, 1 to 2 minutes (it will not be fluffy yet). Beat in the vanilla and salt. Add the room-temperature butter about 2 tablespoons at a time, beating on medium-high the entire time, stopping to scrape the sides of the bowl as needed. (The mixture will become stiff and cold around the edges.) Stop the mixer and remove about ½ cup of the buttercream to a microwave-safe dish.

5. Soften the ½ cup buttercream in the microwave for about 20 seconds or until very soft but not melted. Return the softened buttercream to the mixing bowl and beat in. (This will soften the mixture to a creamy consistency. Repeat this step if necessary.) The buttercream should be fluffy and creamy and easy to spread and

pipe. If the buttercream becomes too soft, chill for about 30 minutes or until the edges begin to firm up. Scrape down the edges of the bowl and beat until creamy. If desired, beat in a very tiny amount of blue food coloring to make the frosting appear whiter and less yellow.

6. To assemble the cake, place the pink cake layer on a serving plate. Spread about ½ cup buttercream frosting over the top of the cake. Place the blue cake layer on top and spread another ½ cup frosting on top. Place the green cake layer on top. Use enough of the remaining frosting to just evenly cover the sides and top of the cake with a thin layer of frosting, using a long metal spatula to smooth the frosting. Reserve about 2 cups of the frosting for decorating the cake.

7. To decorate the cake in a black-and-white cartoon style, tint 1 cup of the reserved frosting black. Tint the remaining 1 cup of the frosting gray. Chill the white frosted cake well so the frosting is firm. With a small metal spatula, spread the gray frosting onto the sides of the cake to create a scalloped design. Place the black frosting in a piping bag fitted with a small round tip. Pipe black outlines around the gray area to create a two-dimensional cartoon effect. Pipe additional designs with black frosting as desired.

Look at all my colors. Don't they make you smile? Visit me in prison. I'll be here for a while!

YIELD: 8 servings
V

Mrs. Smith's Coconut Cream Pie

Well, hello, girls! I'm delighted that your father asked me to share my famous coconut cream pie recipe with you. I'm awfully sorry that we ended up in a huge pie fight that night I served them, thanks to my husband, Harold, being an evil supervillain and all.

Anyway, I think you'll find that this pie is yummy if you actually manage to eat it instead of throwing it. This recipe is for one big pie to share, but I like to make individual pies so that each of my party guests has one just for them.

PECAN SHORTBREAD CRUST
Vegetable oil, for greasing the pie plate
4 tablespoons butter, melted
1½ cups coarsely ground shortbread cookies
¼ cup finely chopped pecans

FILLING
½ cup granulated sugar
¼ cup cornstarch
½ teaspoon salt

One 13.75-ounce can unsweetened coconut milk
1¼ cups whole milk
4 egg yolks
1 teaspoon coconut extract
1 cup finely shredded sweetened coconut

TOPPING
1½ cups heavy whipping cream
2 tablespoons powdered sugar
1 teaspoon vanilla extract
½ cup shredded sweetened coconut, lightly toasted

1. **To make the pecan shortbread crust:** Preheat the oven to 350°F. Grease a 9-inch pie plate with vegetable oil. In a medium bowl, combine the butter, cookie crumbs, and pecans. Press the crust with your fingers or the bottom of a glass into the bottom and all of the way up the sides of the greased pie plate. Bake until very lightly browned and firm, about 10 minutes. Cool slightly, then chill in the refrigerator while you make the filling.

2. **To make the filling:** In a medium saucepan over no heat, combine the granulated sugar, cornstarch, and salt. Pour the coconut milk into a medium bowl and whisk until the solids and liquids are thoroughly combined and the coconut milk is smooth. Gradually whisk the coconut milk and whole milk into the sugar mixture. Bring the mixture to a simmer over medium heat, whisking occasionally. Remove from the heat.

3. In a medium bowl, lightly beat the egg yolks. Slowly add half of the hot coconut mixture, whisking constantly, then whisk in the remaining hot coconut mixture. Return all of the coconut mixture to the saucepan. Return to a simmer over low heat. Cook, whisking constantly, until thickened, about 1 minute. Remove from the heat. Stir in the coconut extract and finely shredded coconut. Pour the filling into the prepared crust. Cover the surface of the filling with plastic wrap. Chill for several hours or until well chilled.

4. **To make the topping:** Just before serving, place the whipping cream in a medium mixing bowl. Add the powdered sugar and vanilla extract. Beat with an electric mixer until soft peaks form, 3 to 4 minutes. Spoon over the chilled pie filling and sprinkle with toasted coconut.

110

Townsville Taffy

You know what they say, girls. You can't end the day without being happy, after biting into a sweet piece of Townsville Taffy!

Remember when your Uncle Eugene came to visit? All he could talk about was taffy. "Gimme gimme gimme! Want taffy!" Gosh, it was almost like he was a furry old taffy monster!

The best thing about Townsville Taffy is that you don't have to visit Townsville to eat it. It's easy to make at home, in all different flavors. If your taffy comes out sweet, with a hint of salt, you've done it right.

2 tablespoons butter, divided

1¼ cups granulated cane sugar (see note)

4 teaspoons cornstarch

½ cup light-colored corn syrup

½ cup water

½ teaspoon sea salt

2 teaspoons your choice of flavoring extract, such as lemon, peppermint, cherry, or root beer

½ teaspoon your choice of concentrated gel food coloring

SPECIAL EQUIPMENT

Candy thermometer

1. Grease two 13-by-9-by-2-inch baking pans or baking dishes with 1 tablespoon butter.

2. In a large heavy saucepan, combine the sugar and cornstarch. Stir in the corn syrup, water, the remaining 1 tablespoon butter, and the salt. Bring to a boil over medium-high heat. Clip a candy thermometer to the side of the pan. Reduce the heat; boil gently, stirring frequently, until the candy reaches 250°F (hard-ball stage). Remove from the heat. Stir in the flavoring extract and food coloring of your choice. Pour the mixture evenly into the prepared pans.

3. Let stand until cool enough to handle, about 10 to 15 minutes. With buttered hands, remove one portion of candy from a pan and stretch and pull into a long piece. Fold in half. Continue to stretch, pull, and fold until lightened in color, about 15 to 30 minutes. (This can take a while and it helps to have help stretching the taffy.) When it has lightened in color, stretch and twist the candy into a long rope about ½ inch thick. Repeat with the other portion of candy. Let cool on a cutting board for a few minutes.

4. Cut the taffy ropes into 1½-inch lengths with a sharp knife. Wrap individual pieces in waxed paper.

Note: It's worth seeking out cane sugar—it's widely available and will be specified on the label. For most candy-making purposes, cane sugar is thought to caramelize better than beet sugar, and beet sugar tends to burn more easily than cane sugar.

You sure are hairy, Uncle Eugene!

Lucky Captain Rabbit King Marshmallow Treats

Girls, I know you love your favorite cereal, Lucky Captain Rabbit King Nuggets. I had an idea: Why not turn your favorite cereal into a dessert? Mix in some melted marshmallows, cut it into shapes, and you have a yummy delight perfect after a long day of school and crime fighting. And don't worry if the grocery store is all out of Lucky Captain Rabbit King cereal—in a pinch, mixing together other popular cereals will do the trick.

Butter or nonstick cooking spray, for greasing the pan

1/2 cup unsalted butter

1/4 teaspoon salt

One 16-ounce package mini marshmallows

One 7-ounce jar marshmallow creme

4 cups oat cereal with marshmallows

2 cups crunchy sweetened corn and oat cereal

2 cups round rice and corn cereal

Rainbow jimmies or other candy decorations (optional)

1. Spray a 9-by-13-by-2-inch baking pan or 3-quart baking dish with nonstick spray.

2. In a large saucepan, melt the butter over low heat. Stir in the salt and marshmallows. Cook and stir until the marshmallows are melted. Remove from the heat and stir in the marshmallow creme until well blended.

Gently stir in the cereals until the cereals are evenly coated. Transfer the mixture to the prepared pan. Press with the back of a spoon to flatten the mixture evenly into the pan. Do not crush the cereal. If desired, sprinkle with jimmies or candy decorations. Cool for several hours or chill for 30 minutes before cutting into bars.

YIELD: About 60 pieces
V+, GF

Irresistible Orange and Pistachio Turkish Delight

Taking control of Townsville was as easy as giving candy to a baby. That dopey Mayor of Townsville turned over the whole town to my daddy for a room full of Turkish Delight. Then Daddy turned the town over to ME! Mayor Princess! I got to make all the rules and tell everybody what to do!

If you want your own town, you'd better not try to take mine. Use this recipe for Turkish Delight candy and find your own chuckleheaded nincompoop who will trade you for it.

Vegetable oil, for greasing the pan

3 cups granulated sugar

2½ cups water, divided

3 tablespoons fresh lemon juice

1 cup cornstarch, divided

¾ teaspoon cream of tartar

1 tablespoon rose water (traditional but optional)

1 teaspoon orange extract

Few drops orange gel food coloring

½ cup finely chopped and sifted pistachios

¼ cup sifted powdered sugar

¼ cup finely shredded sweetened coconut

SPECIAL EQUIPMENT

Candy thermometer

1. Brush an 8-inch square pan with vegetable oil; set aside.

2. In a small saucepan, combine the granulated sugar, 1 cup water, and the lemon juice. Bring to a boil over medium-high heat. Reduce the heat; cook and stir at a simmer until a candy thermometer registers 240°F. Remove the pan from the heat and remove the candy thermometer.

3. In a medium saucepan over no heat, whisk together ¾ cup cornstarch, the cream of tartar, and ¾ cup water. Bring the remaining 1½ cups water to a boil in another small saucepan. Add the boiling water all at once to the cornstarch mixture, whisking to combine. Place the pan over medium heat and cook, stirring constantly for 2 to 3 minutes, until the mixture becomes very thick and just begins to bubble. Pour the syrup mixture into the cornstarch mixture, stirring constantly. Reduce the heat to low and bring the mixture to a simmer. Continue to simmer over low heat for 1 hour and 15 minutes, stirring frequently. Remove from the heat. Stir in the rose water, if using, orange extract, food coloring, and pistachios. Pour into the greased pan and let stand overnight.

4. In a food processor, combine the remaining ¼ cup cornstarch, the powdered sugar, and the coconut. Process with several pulses to chop up the coconut into small pieces. Sprinkle about one-third of the coconut mixture in an even 9-inch square layer on a cutting board. Unmold the candy onto the coconut layer. Sprinkle the top of the candy with about one-third more of the remaining coconut mixture. With a sharp knife, cut the candy into 1-inch squares; separate slightly. Let the candy squares sit uncovered overnight to dry slightly.

5. Before serving, sprinkle with the remaining coconut mixture to coat. Store in an airtight container for up to 2 weeks.

Criminally Good Candy

There was a time, girls, when I tried to forbid you from eating candy. It's terrible for your teeth and can give you a super sugar rush! But when the Mayor gave you candy after saving the town, I wasn't there to stop you. Your insatiable hunger for candy grew faster than a mutant monster!

Since that fateful day, I have realized that forbidding the treat might have been too drastic. Moderation, as they say, is the key. Besides, making your own candy is fun! That's why I'm including my recipe for colorful gummy bites in this cookbook.

Cornstarch, for dusting the candy molds

One 3-ounce box of your desired fruit-flavored gelatin mix

Two ¼-ounce envelopes unflavored gelatin

⅓ cup water

SPECIAL EQUIPMENT

Mini-size (1 to 2 milliliter) silicone candy molds of choice (such as teddy bears, hearts, doughnuts, or stars) for a total of about 100 pieces

Disposable pipette or candy droppers

1. Dust the candy molds with a light coating of cornstarch. (A pastry brush works well to get into tiny corners.) Tap out the excess cornstarch. Set aside.

2. In a small saucepan, stir together the flavored gelatin mix and the unflavored gelatin. Whisk in the water. Let stand for 5 minutes. Place the pan over medium-low heat and whisk constantly until the gelatins are dissolved, about 5 minutes. (A spoon dipped in the mixture should be clear, with no specks.) Remove from the heat.

3. Use a pipette to fill each of the tiny candy molds with the gelatin mixture. Let the filled molds stand for 10 minutes to cool. Dust the tops of the candies with a light coating of cornstarch. (A fine-mesh sieve works well for this.) Chill in the refrigerator for 15 minutes or until firm and set.

4. Place 1 tablespoon cornstarch in a shallow bowl or pie plate. Unmold the candies, one tray at a time, into the bowl. Toss the candies lightly to coat. Store the candies in an airtight container in a cool place or refrigerator for up to 2 weeks.

Mmmm, candy!

Active Volcano Lava Cakes

YIELD: 4 servings

V

I, Mojo Jojo, have returned with a recipe for the most delicious dessert! This dessert was inspired by the site of my supersecret observatory: a volcano.

My observatory sits atop a volcano that overlooks all of Townsville. I once traveled back in time and tried to throw young Professor Utonium into the volcano so he would not grow up to create the Powerpuff Girls, but that is another story.

This is not a story. This is a recipe for a most delicious volcano cake. It has a hot, melted center that is like lava except it is delicious. Because this is a dessert, not a real volcano.

CREAM CHEESE LAVA FROSTING

4 ounces cream cheese, softened

2 tablespoons powdered sugar

1/2 teaspoon vanilla extract

Orange and red gel food coloring, for decorating

CAKES

1/2 cup plus 1 tablespoon butter, divided

Unsweetened cocoa powder, for coating the ramekins

4 ounces bittersweet or semisweet chocolate, chopped

1 1/4 cups powdered sugar

2 whole eggs

3 egg yolks

1 teaspoon vanilla extract

1/2 cup all-purpose flour

SPECIAL EQUIPMENT

Four 6-ounce ramekins or custard cups

1. Preheat the oven to 425°F.

2. **To make the cream cheese lava frosting:** In a small bowl, combine the cream cheese, powdered sugar, and vanilla until smooth. Remove about half of the frosting to another small bowl. Tint one bowl orange and the other bowl red with gel food coloring. Stir together just until swirled, with streaks of color remaining.

3. **To make the cakes:** Grease four 6-ounce ramekins or custard cups with 1 tablespoon butter. Sprinkle the greased cups with some cocoa powder to coat (a small fine-mesh sieve works well for this). Tap out any excess cocoa powder. Set aside.

4. In a large microwave-safe bowl, microwave the remaining 1/2 cup butter and the chocolate on high for 1 minute. Stir to blend. If the chocolate is still not melted, microwave for another 30 seconds. Do not overheat the chocolate. Stir in the powdered sugar until well blended. Whisk in the eggs, egg yolks, and vanilla. Whisk in the flour. Divide the batter evenly among the prepared ramekins. Place the ramekins on a baking sheet and bake until the edges are firm and the centers are still soft, about 13 minutes.

5. Run a small sharp knife around the inside edges of the ramekins to be sure the cakes don't stick. While still hot, and using pot holders, invert the cakes onto serving plates. Dollop the tops of the cakes with cream cheese lava frosting and serve while still very warm.

Blossom's Ice Breath Treats

When it's hot out, I collaborate with Blossom to make snow cones in a flash! But you don't *need* ice breath to make snow cones. All you need is a freezer and a food processor. It might take a little longer than using superpowers to make them, but the end result will taste just as good.

4 cups frozen pitted sweet or tart cherries

1 cup granulated sugar

1 cup water

1 wide-strip lime peel, about 4 inches long

2 teaspoons fresh lime juice

3 cups ice cubes

Lime slices, for garnish (optional)

SPECIALTY EQUIPMENT

Paper snow cone cups

1. In a large saucepan, combine the cherries, sugar, water, lime peel, and lime juice. Cook and stir over medium heat until the sugar is dissolved and the cherries are mostly thawed, 2 to 3 minutes. Mash the cherries with a potato masher to break up the fruit. Simmer and stir for about 10 minutes or until the fruit has broken down into a chunky sauce. Remove from the heat and cool to room temperature.

2. Place a fine-mesh sieve over a medium bowl. Pour the cherry mixture through the sieve to remove the fruit chunks. Transfer the syrup to a bottle with a pouring spout or a squeeze bottle. Store in the refrigerator until ready to use.

3. To make crushed ice, place about 3 cups ice cubes in a blender or food processor. Blend or process with pulses until the ice is crushed into small pieces, stopping to scrape down the sides of the blender as needed. Immediately scoop the crushed ice into paper cones or cups. Drizzle with the cherry syrup and garnish with a lime slice. Make more batches of crushed ice as needed.

It's worth the brain freeze!

Sugar, Spice, and Everything Nice Snack Cake

It seems fitting to include a recipe with the ingredients that started everything: sugar, spice, and everything nice. This time, I've adjusted the formula to result in a light and fluffy snack cake instead of three perfect little girls.

Lemon makes this cake's frosting extra nice, powdered ginger adds some spice, and molasses adds a rich sweetness. But no cake, no matter how good, will ever be as sweet as you three girls!

CAKE

Vegetable oil, for greasing the pan

1½ cups all-purpose flour

½ teaspoon baking soda

1 teaspoon ground ginger

½ teaspoon ground cinnamon

¼ teaspoon ground cloves

¼ teaspoon salt

½ cup unsalted butter, room temperature

½ cup packed brown sugar

1 large egg

½ cup molasses

½ cup lukewarm water (about 95°F)

Whipped cream, for garnish

Thinly sliced lemon, for garnish

LEMON SYRUP GLAZE

1 cup granulated sugar

½ cup water

1 teaspoon lemon zest

2 tablespoons lemon juice

1. **To make the cake:** Preheat the oven to 350°F. Grease an 8-inch square cake pan with vegetable oil. Line the bottom of the pan with parchment paper; set aside. In a medium mixing bowl, whisk together the flour, baking soda, ginger, cinnamon, cloves, and salt.

2. In a large mixing bowl, beat the butter with an electric mixer on medium speed for 30 seconds. Add the brown sugar and beat until fluffy. Add the egg and molasses and beat for 1 minute. Alternately add the flour mixture and lukewarm water in batches, beating until combined after each addition. Scrape the sides of the bowl as needed to combine. Pour the batter into the prepared pan.

3. Bake until a toothpick inserted in the center of the cake comes out clean, 30 to 35 minutes.

4. **To make the lemon syrup glaze:** In a small saucepan, combine the sugar and water. Bring to a boil over medium-high heat. Simmer for 2 minutes. Let cool completely. Stir in the lemon zest and lemon juice.

5. When the cake is done, place on a wire rack to cool for 5 minutes. Loosen the sides of the warm cake from the pan with a knife or metal spatula. Pour half of the lemon syrup glaze over the cake in the pan. Let the cake stand for 5 to 10 minutes to soak up the glaze. Serve the cake wedges warm or cooled with a drizzle of some of the remaining glaze and a dollop of whipped cream. Garnish with lemon slices.

Signal-in-the-Sky Sweethearts

Things might look grim in the city of Townsville when a giant monster attacks or alien ships attack with laser beams. But in times of trouble, a sign of hope appears: a heart-shaped beacon gleams in the darkness, alerting you girls that help is needed.

This beacon gives so many a sense of hope so sweet that I thought: *Why not re-create it as a cookie?* A basic sugar cookie recipe, a heart-shaped cookie cutter, and colored frosting is all you need.

COOKIES

One 1.2-ounce package freeze-dried strawberries

2/3 cup unsalted butter, softened

3/4 cup granulated sugar

1 teaspoon baking powder

1/4 teaspoon salt

1 large egg

1 teaspoon vanilla extract

2 teaspoons lemon zest

1 tablespoon lemon juice

Red gel food coloring, for decorating

2 cups all-purpose flour, plus more for the work surface

LEMON ICING

2 cups sifted powdered sugar

1 tablespoon lemon juice

1 to 2 tablespoons milk

Red gel food coloring, for decorating

SPECIAL EQUIPMENT

2 1/2 - to 3-inch heart-shaped cookie cutter

Decorating bag or small food-storage bag

1. **To make the cookies:** Place the dried strawberries in a small food processor or compact blender. Blend or process into a powder. In a large mixing bowl, beat the butter with an electric mixer for 30 seconds. Add the sugar, baking powder, and salt. Beat on high speed for 2 minutes, until fluffy. Beat in the egg until well combined. Beat in the vanilla, lemon zest, lemon juice, and strawberry powder. Beat in enough red food coloring to make your desired pink color. Scrape the sides of the bowl. Beat in as much of the flour as you can with the mixer. Stir in the remaining flour. Shape the dough into a flat disk. Wrap the dough in plastic wrap and chill for about 30 minutes or until easy to handle.

2. Preheat the oven to 350°F. Line a baking sheet with parchment paper. On a floured surface, roll the dough to 1/4-inch thickness. Use the heart-shaped cookie cutter to cut out shapes. Place the cookies 1 inch apart on the prepared baking sheet. Bake until the centers are firm, 8 to 10 minutes. Transfer the cookies to a wire rack to cool completely.

3. **To make the lemon icing:** In a bowl, combine the powdered sugar, lemon juice, and milk to make a smooth icing that will drizzle from a spoon but will stay on the cookie. Remove about 1/3 cup of the icing to a small bowl. Add red gel food coloring to get a color that matches the cookies. Place the colored icing in a decorating bag or small food-storage bag. Twist bag shut.

4. Working with a few cookies at a time, spread the untinted lemon icing over the tops of the cookies, spreading to about 1/4 inch from the edges of the cookies. Snip a small opening from the tip of the decorating bag with colored icing. Pipe two concentric hearts on top of each iced cookie. Repeat with the remaining cookies.

Jumbo Mintz

You girls certainly are resourceful. I was very impressed when you tried to stop the Gangreen Gang from buying a Destruct-o-Ray at Mojo Jojo's garage sale. To raise money, you girls whipped up a batch of chocolate-and-peppermint cookies and sold them door-to-door.

I've been craving those crunchy cookies. I hope you'll use this recipe to whip up a batch for your old pops!

COOKIES

1 cup unsweetened dark cocoa powder

1 cup sifted powdered sugar

3/4 teaspoon salt

1 1/2 cups all-purpose flour

1 cup unsalted butter, room temperature

1 teaspoon mint extract

CHOCOLATE-MINT COATING

One 16-ounce good-quality chocolate melting disks

2 teaspoons vegetable shortening or coconut oil, plus more as needed

1/2 teaspoon mint extract

Green and white nonpareils, for decorating

SPECIAL EQUIPMENT

3- to 3 1/2-inch round cookie cutter

1. **To make the cookies:** In a food processor, combine the cocoa powder, powdered sugar, salt, and flour. Process for a few seconds, until well combined. Add the butter and mint extract. Process with on and off pulses until the dough just begins to hold together. Remove the dough from the food processor and press into a flat disk. Wrap the disk in plastic wrap and chill for 30 minutes.

2. Preheat the oven to 350°F; line two baking sheets with parchment paper. On a lightly floured surface, roll out the dough to a thin even layer, 1/8 inch thick. Use the cookie cutter to cut out shapes and place them 1 inch apart on the prepared baking sheets. Bake for 8 to 10 minutes or until firm. Let cool for a few minutes before transferring to a wire rack to cool.

3. **To make the chocolate-mint coating:** Place the chocolate melting disks in a medium bowl over a pot of simmering water or double boiler. (The bottom of the bowl should not touch the simmering water.) Heat the chocolate, stirring occasionally, until completely melted. Stir in the shortening and mint extract. (The melted chocolate should be a little thin and drizzle from a spoon. If it's too thick, add another teaspoon of shortening.)

4. Place a piece of parchment paper on a work surface. Using a fork, lower a cookie into the melted chocolate, turning over to coat both sides. Lift the cookie out of the chocolate, right-side up, and tap on the top edge of the bowl to shed any excess chocolate. Remove the excess chocolate from the bottom of the cookie by swiping it along the top edge of the bowl. Place the cookie on the parchment paper. Sprinkle the top of each cookie with a few green and white sprinkles. Repeat to thinly coat the remaining cookies with chocolate. Let the dipped cookies cool until set. (If the room is warm, place the cookies and their parchment paper on a baking sheet and chill in the refrigerator for 15 minutes.)

5. When set, peel the cookies from the parchment paper. Store in an airtight container in a cool, dry place for up to 2 weeks.

The Mayor's Wife's Chocolate Chip Cookies and Milk

Why, hello there! My dear husband is the Mayor of Townsville, and he works very hard indeed. Why, when he comes home, he's always muttering about something (usually monsters or pickles), and he only has time to play four hours of video games before he falls asleep in his chair. While he plays, he asks for his favorite snack: chocolate chip cookies.

And my, can that man eat chocolate chip cookies! He'll gobble down two dozen in a sitting. That keeps me busy baking every day, but I don't mind. I love that Mayor of mine!

1 cup unsalted butter, room temperature	4 egg yolks or 1 egg and 1 yolk
⅔ cup granulated sugar	3 tablespoons milk, plus more for serving
⅔ cup packed brown sugar	1 tablespoon vanilla extract
1 teaspoon salt	2½ cups cake flour
½ teaspoon baking soda	10 ounces chopped bittersweet chocolate or milk chocolate

1. Preheat the oven to 350°F. Line a baking sheet with parchment paper. In the bowl of a stand mixer or a large mixing bowl if using a hand mixer, beat the butter for 30 seconds or until very soft. Add the granulated sugar, brown sugar, salt, and baking soda. Beat on medium-high until fluffy, about 3 minutes. Beat in the egg yolks, milk, and vanilla. Add the flour. Beat on low until well combined, scraping the sides of the bowl as needed. Stir in the chocolate.

2. With a spoon or cookie scoop, drop 2 tablespoons of dough 2 inches apart on the prepared baking sheet. Flatten the mounds of dough to a ¼-inch thickness using a fork. Bake until golden brown and crispy, 12 to 15 minutes. Let the cookies cool for a few minutes before transferring to a wire rack to cool completely. Repeat with the remaining dough, replacing the parchment paper when it begins to show oil spots. Serve the cookies on top of a glass of milk.

THIS RECIPE MAKES CRISPY COOKIES, JUST LIKE I LIKE 'EM.

Stash o' Nuts Brittle

Girls, I've invented a new holiday: Nuts Day, the day we celebrate when you girls saved the town from mad squirrels. Bubbles, you used your ability to speak squirrel to figure out why the squirrels were so angry. A new statue of the Mayor had covered up the hole used by the town's squirrels to store their nuts!

I was inspired to formulate this recipe so that we can celebrate Nuts Day every year. This crunchy brittle contains three different kinds of nuts. Just remember, it's for humans only. Squirrels should not eat candy.

¼ cup unsalted butter, plus more butter, softened, for greasing the pans

2 cups granulated cane sugar (see note, page 111)

½ cup honey

½ cup light-colored corn syrup

½ cup water

2½ cups mixed nuts, such as peanuts, cashews, pecan halves, whole almonds, pepitas

1½ teaspoons baking soda

SPECIALTY EQUIPMENT

Candy thermometer

1. Grease two large baking pans with some of the softened butter. Butter the sides of a 3-quart heavy saucepan. In the saucepan, combine the sugar, honey, corn syrup, water, and ¼ cup butter. Cook and stir over medium-high heat until the mixture comes to a boil, stirring occasionally. Clip a candy thermometer to the pan. Reduce the heat to medium-low. Continue to maintain a gentle boil until the thermometer registers 275°F, about 30 minutes, stirring frequently.

2. Stir in the nuts. Continue to cook and stir at a gentle boil until the thermometer registers 295°F, about 10 minutes. Remove the pan from the heat and remove the thermometer from the pan. Quickly stir in the baking soda and stir well until combined. (The mixture will bubble up and become lighter in color.) Immediately pour the hot mixture into the prepared pans. Be careful not to touch the hot brittle with your hands. Working quickly, use two forks to pull the edges of the brittle sheets outward to make thinner layers. Cool completely; break into pieces. Store in an airtight container for up to 1 week.

Once again, Bubbles and Bullet save the day!

The Mayor's Can't-Stop-at-a-Slice Cherry Pie

Oh, sweet, sweet cherry pie! I can't resist it. Once, I ate four whole cherry pies at my desk. Ms. Bellum had to pry those pie tins out of my sticky hands. Boy, did I make a mess!

Ms. Bellum doesn't let me eat cherry pies in the office anymore. That's why I need you girls to help. Maybe you could bake me one (or two or three) and sneak them into the office for me? Just be careful not to have a slice before you bring them over. If you're like me, you won't be able to stop!

LATTICE PIECRUST

2 cups all-purpose flour

½ teaspoon salt

½ cup cold butter, sliced

½ cup shortening

FILLING

5 to 6 cups pitted tart cherries, fresh or frozen

1½ cups granulated sugar

3 tablespoons quick tapioca or
4 tablespoons cornstarch

1 teaspoon vanilla or almond extract

Pinch salt

All-purpose flour, for the work surface

1 tablespoon butter

1 egg, beaten

1. **To make the lattice piecrust:** In a large bowl, combine the all-purpose flour and salt. Using a pastry blender or your fingers, cut in the butter and shortening. Continue to work the dough until the butter and shortening form pea-size clumps. Drizzle a few tablespoons of ice water over the flour mixture and toss with a fork to moisten. Continue to add more water a few tablespoons at a time, using only as much water as needed to make a dough that will hold together in a ball (⅓ to ½ cup total). Press the dough into a ball. Divide the ball in half. Wrap each portion in plastic wrap and chill until needed.

2. **To make the filling:** Partially thaw the cherries, if frozen. In a large bowl, combine the cherries, sugar, tapioca, vanilla, and salt. Let stand for 20 minutes.

3. Preheat the oven to 425°F. On a lightly floured surface, roll out one-half of the chilled dough to a 12-inch circle. Transfer the circle to a 9-inch pie plate. Ease the dough into the bottom of the plate without stretching the dough. Transfer the cherry mixture to the pie plate. Cut the butter into small pieces and place on top of the cherry mixture.

4. On a floured surface, roll out the remaining half of dough to a 12-inch circle. Cut the dough into 1-inch-wide strips. Place the strips on top of the cherry filling in a lattice pattern, weaving the strips over and under one another. Trim the edge of the piecrust to 1 inch beyond the edge of the pie plate. Roll up the piecrust edges and pinch together to seal. Crimp the edges as desired. Brush the top crust with the beaten egg.

5. Bake at 425°F for 15 minutes. Reduce the heat to 375°F and bake until the filling is bubbly and the crust is browned, an additional 30 to 40 minutes (40 to 50 minutes for frozen cherries). Cool completely before cutting.

Surprise Party Cupcakes

I may be a good baker, but I am a terrible artist! Once, I tried to surprise you girls with cakes decorated to look like you. When I tried to replace the cakes, you girls thought I was going to try to replace you. You were so upset that you blew up my lab—but I forgave you.

To make sure nothing like that ever happens again, I created this recipe. It's much easier to make cupcakes that look like you!

CUPCAKES

2 cups all-purpose flour

2 teaspoons baking powder

1/2 teaspoon baking soda

1/2 teaspoon salt

1/2 cup plus 2 tablespoons unsalted butter, room temperature

1 cup granulated sugar

2 large eggs

2 teaspoons vanilla extract

1 1/3 cups buttermilk

1/4 cup rainbow sprinkles

2 cups white buttercream frosting

MARSHMALLOW FONDANT

One 16-ounce package mini marshmallows

1/4 cup water

1 teaspoon vanilla extract

1/4 cup unsalted butter

2 pounds sifted powdered sugar, divided

Gel food coloring in green, blue, yellow, pink, orange, black, red, and peach or flesh color

1. Preheat the oven to 375°F. Line 18 standard muffin cups with paper liners.

2. **To make the cupcakes:** In a medium bowl, stir together the flour, baking powder, baking soda, and salt. In a large bowl, using an electric mixer, beat together the butter and sugar on medium-high until light and fluffy, about 3 minutes. Add the eggs one at a time, beating well after each addition. Add the vanilla and beat until blended. Turn off the mixer and scrape down the bowl with a rubber spatula. Add about half of the flour mixture and beat on low speed just until combined. Then add the buttermilk and beat just until combined. Add the remaining flour mixture and beat just until combined. Turn off the mixer, scrape down the bowl, and add the rainbow sprinkles. Stir just until combined.

3. Use an ice-cream scoop or a spoon to place the batter into the cupcake liners, filling them about two-thirds full. Bake until light golden brown and a toothpick inserted into the center of the cupcake comes out clean, about 17 minutes. Let the cupcakes cool in pans on a wire rack for 10 minutes. Carefully transfer the cupcakes to the rack and cool completely.

4. Spread a thin layer of frosting over the tops of the cupcakes.

5. **To make the marshmallow fondant:** Place the marshmallows in a large microwave-safe bowl and microwave on high to start melting the marshmallows, 30 to 60 seconds. Add the water, vanilla, and butter. Stir until the marshmallows and butter are melted and the mixture is smooth. Stir or beat in the powdered sugar, 1 cup at a time, until the mixture makes a very stiff, sticky dough that forms a ball. Place the remaining powdered sugar on a work surface and turn out the fondant. Knead the dough with your hands, working in the powdered sugar, until the fondant dough is smooth and no longer sticky. Wrap the fondant in plastic wrap and let rest overnight.

6. When ready to use, knead the fondant again in a little powdered sugar to soften. To make the Powerpuff Girls' faces, tint small amounts of fondant green, blue, yellow, pink, orange, black, red, and peach or flesh color. For each color, take a ball of fondant (1 to 2 inches) and add a few drops of desired food coloring. Wearing disposable plastic gloves, knead in the food coloring until it's your desired color. Keep the fondant wrapped in plastic when not using.

7. On a surface lightly dusted with powdered sugar, roll out the colored fondant to about 1/8- to 1/16-inch thickness. Use tiny cutters, straws, or a sharp knife to cut out circles and other shapes needed to make faces, eyes, and hair. Assemble the faces and place on top of the frosted cupcakes.

Patterns

Face and Eyes

Eye Color Guide

Blossom

Buttercup

Bubbles

Dietary Considerations

V = Vegetarian
V+ = Vegan
GF = Gluten-Free

CHAPTER ONE: POWER-UP BREAKFAST AND BRUNCH

Protein Power Pancakes: V

Monster Avocado Toast: V

Bubbles's Microwave Soufflé: V

Spicy-Hot Savory Oatmeal: V, GF

Mojo-in-the-Hole

Bagel Boy Breakfast Sandwich

Brikowski's Favorite Glazed: V

Super Energy Smoothies: V, GF

The Mayor's Brioche Toast with Sweet Cherry Jam: V

CHAPTER TWO: AWESOME APPETIZERS AND AFTER-SCHOOL SNACKS

The Mayor's Favorite Fried Pickles: V

Sedusa's Date-Night Turnovers: V

Ima Goodlady's Sweet-as-Apple-Pie Turnovers: V

Imposter Octi Bread

Rowdyruff Boys' Snips and Snails and Puppy Dog Tails Snack Mix: V

Mopey Popo's Banana Chips: V+, GF

Powerpuff Cheese and Sausage Selection

Bow Wow Wow Snack Mix: V, GF

HIM's Devilishly Good Dip: V, GF

Nano Nuggets

Pretzel Day Pretzel Bites: V

CHAPTER THREE: MIGHTY MAINS AND SUPERHERO SIDES

Beef and Hog Dogs

Superhero Picnic Sandwiches

The Ministry of Pain's "Feast of Villainy"

Accidental Sloppy Joes

#1 Chef Shrimp and Tuna Teppanyaki

Anti–Gangreen Gang Field (Trip) Greens: V, GF

Father's Day Steaks with Onion–Red Wine Gravy

Chicken Soup for the Criminally Incompetent

Valentine's Day Meatloaf

Ms. Keane's Alphabet Soup

Pizza Pie Laboratory Special

The Mayor's Naked Spaghetti: V

Professor's Prizewinning Chili: GF

Salami Swami's Antipasto Salad: GF

Maid Mary's Happy Stew

Eat 'Em to Beat 'Em Broccoli with Cheese Sauce: V

All-of-the-Oranges Salad: V+, GF

CHAPTER FOUR: DARING DRINKS

Chemical X-cellent: V+, GF

Fuzzy Lumpkins's "Get Offa Mah Property" Spicy Ginger-Grapefruit Punch: V+, GF

Princess Morbucks's Fancy Water on the Rocks: V+, GF

"Sand-Sprinkled" Chamomile Latte: V+, GF

Bubbles's Boffo Bubble Tea: V, GF

The Mayor's "Singing" Apple Juice Sipper: V+, GF

Moejisha's Special Secret Recipe "Tea": V, GF

CHAPTER FIVE: DOMINATING DESSERTS

Townsville Ice-Cream Truck Treats: V

Le Dunne King Donnet's 5-Star Doughnuts: V

Mr. Mime's Black-and-White Cake: V

Mrs. Smith's Coconut Cream Pie: V

Townsville Taffy: V, GF

Lucky Captain Rabbit King Marshmallow Treats: V

Irresistible Orange and Pistachio Turkish Delight: V+, GF

Criminally Good Candy: GF

Active Volcano Lava Cakes: V

Blossom's Ice Breath Treats: V+, GF

Sugar, Spice, and Everything Nice Snack Cake: V

Signal-in-the-Sky Sweethearts: V

Jumbo Mintz: V

The Mayor's Wife's Chocolate Chip Cookies and Milk: V

Stash o' Nuts Brittle: V, GF

The Mayor's Can't-Stop-at-a-Slice Cherry Pie: V

Surprise Party Cupcakes: V

Fry Station Safety Tips

If you're making something that requires deep-frying, here are some important tips to prevent any kitchen fires:

- If you don't have a dedicated deep fryer, use a Dutch oven or a high-walled sauté pan.
- Never have too much oil in the pan! You don't want hot oil spilling out as soon as you put the food in.
- Only use a suitable cooking oil, like canola, peanut, or vegetable oil.
- Always keep track of the oil temperature with a thermometer—350°F to 375°F should do the trick.
- Never put too much food in the pan at the same time!
- Never put wet food in the pan. It will splatter and may cause burns.
- Always have a lid nearby to cover the pan in case it starts to spill over or catch fire. A properly rated fire extinguisher is also great to have on hand in case of emergencies.
- Never leave the pan unattended and never let children near the pan.
- Never, ever put any body part in the hot oil.

Glossary

COOKING TERMS

Beat: To blend ingredients and/or incorporate air into a mixture by vigorously whisking, stirring, or using a handheld or stand mixer.

Crimp: To seal together the edges of two pieces of pastry dough by pressing the dough with the tines of a kitchen fork, the side of a knife, or a pastry crimper. Crimping is a good way to seal together securely the uncooked crusts of a double-crust pie, which may then be fluted if desired.

Emulsify: This refers to the process of combining two ingredients that do not typically mix easily, such as oil and vinegar.

Folding in: This refers to gently adding an ingredient with a spatula in wide gentle strokes. Do not whisk or stir vigorously. Folding allows any airiness already established to stay intact.

Greasing a pan: Coating a pan with nonstick cooking spray, oil, softened butter, or shortening to keep (usually) baked goods such as cakes from sticking.

Knead: Uncover the dough and knead it by using the heel of one hand to push the dough away from you and then pull it back with your fingertips. Turn and repeat until the dough is smooth and elastic, 5 to 7 minutes.

Mince: Gather the leaves together and rock the blade over them until they are chopped into small, even pieces (finely chopped), or into pieces as fine as possible (minced).

Muddle: A short-handled tool that is textured on one end and used to mash together ingredients such as fruits, herbs, and sugar when making flavored drinks.

Piping frosting: The process of decorating cakes and cookies by squeezing frosting placed in a decorating bag over them. Piping can be done with or without a decorating tip—or even in a plastic bag with one corner snipped off to allow the frosting to be applied in a neat rope shape.

Reduce: Simmering or boiling a liquid, such as broth or wine, is a good way to enhance flavor. As you do so, the quantity of the liquid decreases, and the liquid thickens into a flavorful sauce.

Rise: Traditionally, bread dough rises two times, but sometimes you have to change your habits and ignore logic. Sometimes, as with overnight rolls, I have a very long first rise followed by a shorter rising after shaping. Some of the sourdough breads rest for only a short while before shaping and then rise much longer in the second stage instead. The important point is that the dough is well risen when it's time to bake it. You can always slow down the rising by keeping the dough cool. It is difficult to recommend exact timings but, for example, dough that I let rise for two hours at room temperature might take twice as long when refrigerated. You have to experiment. Another aspect of rising to keep in mind is that a firm dough usually rises more slowly than a moist dough.

Roast: Roasting meats and poultry in an uncovered roasting pan in a hot oven intensifies their flavors. Because the oven does most of the work, this technique requires little hands-on cooking time. Before you start, line a heavy roasting pan with aluminum foil and brush the foil with a little olive oil to help prevent sticking.

INGREDIENTS

Active dry yeast: Available in $\frac{1}{4}$-ounce (7-gram) packages containing $2\frac{1}{4}$ teaspoons yeast. Be sure to check the date on the package to make sure the yeast is truly active. Contrary to what the package says, you don't have to use warm water.

Cake flour: Milled from soft wheat and containing cornstarch, cake flour is low in protein and high in starch. It gives cakes a light crumb. Cake flour has also undergone a bleaching process that increases its ability to hold water and sugar, so cakes made with cake flour are less likely to fall.

Granulated sugar: A highly refined sugar made from sugarcane or beets known for its white color and fine texture. All the molasses has been removed from this type of sugar.

Instant yeast: A third kind of active dry yeast, instant dried yeast, is three times more powerful than active dry yeast. Also called European yeast, it is a stronger, more stable yeast developed for commercial bakers. Some bakers feel that it has an objectionable taste, and it should not be used in sweet bread doughs or those that require long, slow risings.

Salt: Unless otherwise noted, use your salt of choice in the recipes in this book. Kosher salt—which is coarser than regular table salt—is the type of salt that is most commonly used throughout the book.

Vanilla paste vs. vanilla extract: Vanilla bean paste provides strong vanilla flavor and beautiful vanilla bean flecks without having to split and scrape a vanilla bean. Although it is more expensive than extract, there are situations in which it really elevates the finished dish. When that's the case, a recipe will specifically call for vanilla bean paste, but it can always be replaced in a 1-to-1 ratio with vanilla extract.

COOKING UTENSILS

Baking dish: Shallow, rectangular dishes made of tempered glass, porcelain, or earthenware are all-purpose vessels that work for roasting meat or vegetables and baking brownies or bread pudding. Items will cook more slowly in opaque ceramic than they will in clear glass.

Baking pan: Use these pans, which typically measure 13-by-9-inches with sides 2 to $2\frac{1}{2}$ inches high, for baking sheet cakes, brownies, corn bread, and coffee cakes. You can also use these pans for making casseroles.

Baking sheet: A baking sheet (also called a sheet pan) is a rectangular metal pan with shallow, slightly sloping rims. Choose sturdy stainless-steel ones that will last for years.

Blender: Blends or purées sauces and soups to varying textures, from chunky to perfectly smooth. Also used to make smoothies and shakes.

Cake pan: Round pans, generally 2 inches deep and 8 or 9 inches in diameter, used especially for baking cakes. You will want to have at least two on hand for making layer cakes.

Candy thermometer: Sometimes called fry thermometers, these long glass thermometers can be clipped to the side of a pot. They can withstand temperatures of at least 500°F and are used to measure the temperatures of frying oil or sugar when making syrups, candies, and certain frostings.

Dry measuring cups: Measuring tools that usually come in sizes of ¼ cup, ⅓ cup, ½ cup, and 1 cup. They are ideal for measuring dry ingredients such as flour, sugar, rice, and pasta.

Dutch oven: A large heavy cooking pot usually made of cast iron. This can go on the stove or in the oven and is great at retaining heat, making it the perfect cooking vessel for just about everything.

Food processor: An electronic kitchen tool that consists of a plastic bowl fitted over a set of spinning blades, which can be used to assist in a variety of food prep, including chopping, shredding, pulverizing, mixing, and more. Usually comes with at least two speeds and a pulse option to create short bursts of processing. More commonly (but not exclusively) used to prep dry ingredients before cooking.

Frying pan: Shallow round cooking vessel used primarily for stovetop cooking. It's good to have a range of sizes. Generally, a small frying pan or skillet is 6 inches across, a medium skillet is 8 inches across, a large skillet is 10 inches across, and an extra-large skillet is 12 inches across.

High-heat vs. nonstick pans: A high-heat pan—as its name suggests—can stand up to high-heat cooking, generally temperatures between 400°F and 600°F. They're usually made of stainless steel, cast iron, or enameled cast iron and can be used on the stovetop or oven—if the handle is made of an ovenproof material. Nonstick cookware contains a coating that helps keep foods from sticking (particularly eggs), but they can't be used at the same temperatures as high-heat pans. If you are cooking with nonstick cookware, make sure you know the manufacturer's heat limits for your cookware. Most nonstick cookware should not be used at above medium heat on a stovetop (about 350°F) and is not generally suitable for the oven.

Immersion blender: Also called hand or handheld blenders, immersion blenders have an extended blade that is immersed in a food or mixture to blend or purée it. Immersion blenders are great for puréeing food in the container in which it is mixed or cooked. This means that they can blend larger amounts of food than will fit in the jar of a standing blender. Immersion blenders also tend to incorporate more air into a liquid and as such can be used to make a frothy foam on creamed soups. These blenders usually have only two speeds, and the blade must be completely immersed in the food to prevent spattering. Many are designed to hang in a wall mount for easy storage. Some have whisk attachments or small containers for blending smaller amounts of food.

Liquid measuring cup: Clear glass or plastic measuring tools used for measuring precise amounts of liquids by lining up the level of liquid to the marks on the cup. Useful sizes include 1 cup, 2 cup, and 4 cup.

Measuring spoons: A set of measuring tools used to accurately portion smaller amounts of ingredients. They usually come in a set that includes ⅛ teaspoon, ¼ teaspoon, ½ teaspoon, 1 teaspoon, and 1 tablespoon. They can be used for liquid ingredients such as vinegar, juices, oils, and extracts, and dry ingredients such as flour, salt, sugar, and spices.

Mixer: Two basic types of motor-driven electric mixers are available, stand or standing and handheld or portable, and each has its place in the kitchen. Stand mixers are stationary machines good for large amounts and heavy batters.

Parchment paper: Food-safe paper that can withstand temperatures of up to 450°F—even up to 500°F for short baking times—that's used to line pans for baking and roasting. Parchment paper keeps foods from sticking and makes cleanup easier.

Pastry bag: A pastry bag is a cone-shaped bag that is usually used to pipe frosting or icing on cakes, cookies, cupcakes, and other desserts. These come in disposable and reusable options and usually come with a set of attachable tips to create different shapes in your frosting. Some disposable options are microwave-safe, which is useful for melting chocolate or other items (be sure to check the packaging before trying this). Aside from decorating desserts, they can also be used to pipe batter, dough, creams, or puréed ingredients ahead of cooking.

Rolling pin: A long cylindrical tool—most often made of wood—used to flatten and roll out dough when making breads and pastries.

Rubber spatula: A handled tool with a flat flexible blade used to fold ingredients together and to scrape the sides of bowls clean.

Saucepan: This simple round pan has either straight or slightly sloping sides and generally ranges in size from 1 to 5 quarts. If you are buying only one, consider a 2-quart saucepan, which is most versatile. The pans are designed to facilitate rapid evaporation so that a sauce thickens and cooks efficiently. Straight-sided pans with high sides are ideal for longer cooking, since the liquid will not evaporate as quickly.

Silicone baking mat: Used to line shallow baking pans when making foods such as cookies and pastries to prevent sticking. They can withstand high temperatures in the oven and can also be used in the freezer. Dough can be rolled out on them, and they can easily go from prep station to chilling to the oven without having to move the dough. They are easy to clean and reusable.

Skillet: Also called a frying pan, this broad pan is often confused with a sauté pan, but traditionally differs in that it has sides that flare outward, making it useful for cooking foods that must be stirred or turned out of the pan. Most kitchens should have both a smaller one, 9 or 10 inches across the bottom, and a larger one, 12 or 14 inches. Skillets do not have lids. The best materials are anodized aluminum or cast iron; if you buy two, make one of them nonstick.

Spatula/pancake turner: A handled tool with a wide flexible blade used to flip or turn foods during cooking.

Stand mixer: A heavy-duty machine with a large bowl and various attachments used to mix, beat, or whip foods at varying speeds. Stand mixers are necessary for making heavy, dense, or stiff doughs for cookies or yeasted breads.

Whisk: A handled tool with thin wires arranged in various shapes used for mixing and whipping liquids and batters to combine ingredients or incorporate air into them. The two most common types of whisks are the balloon whisk, which has a bulbous end that narrows down toward the handle, and the sauce whisk, which has a round coil that sits flat on the bottom of the pan.

Wok: This versatile Chinese pan is ideal for stir-frying, deep-frying, and steaming. Traditionally made of plain carbon steel, the wok has a rounded bottom that allows small pieces of food to be rapidly tossed and stirred. It also has high, gradually sloping sides to help keep food circulating inside the pan during stir-frying. In Western kitchens, round-bottomed woks are held in place over gas burners by a metal ring that allows the flames to rise and distribute heat around the pan. Woks with flat bottoms have also been developed to sit securely and distribute heat more efficiently on electric burners. Woks can have one long and one short handle, or two short handles, depending on the manufacturer. They are sometimes sold with a lid for steaming.

Conversion Tables

KITCHEN MEASUREMENTS

CUP	TABLESPOON	TEASPOON	FLUID OUNCES
$1/16$ cup	1 tablespoon	3 teaspoons	$1/2$ fluid ounce
$1/8$ cup	2 tablespoons	6 teaspoons	1 fluid ounce
$1/4$ cup	4 tablespoons	12 teaspoons	2 fluid ounces
$1/3$ cup	$5\,1/3$ tablespoons	16 teaspoons	$2\,2/3$ fluid ounces
$1/2$ cup	8 tablespoons	24 teaspoons	4 fluid ounces
$2/3$ cup	$10\,2/3$ tablespoons	32 teaspoons	$5\,1/3$ fluid ounces
$3/4$ cup	12 tablespoons	36 teaspoons	6 fluid ounces
1 cup	16 tablespoons	48 teaspoons	8 fluid ounces

GALLON	QUART	PINT	CUP	FLUID OUNCES
$1/16$ gallon	$1/4$ quart	$1/2$ pint	1 cup	8 fluid ounces
$1/8$ gallon	$1/2$ quart	1 pint	2 cups	16 fluid ounces
$1/4$ gallon	1 quart	2 pints	4 cups	32 fluid ounces
$1/2$ gallon	2 quarts	4 pints	8 cups	64 fluid ounces
1 gallon	4 quarts	8 pints	16 cups	128 fluid ounces

OVEN TEMPERATURES

CELCIUS	FAHRENHEIT
93°C	200°F
107°C	225°F
121°C	250°F
135°C	275°F
149°C	300°F
163°C	325°F
177°C	350°F
191°C	375°F
204°C	400°F
218°C	425°F
232°C	450°F

WEIGHT

GRAMS	OUNCES
14 grams	$1/2$ ounce
28 grams	1 ounce
57 grams	2 ounces
85 grams	3 ounces
113 grams	4 ounces
142 grams	5 ounces
170 grams	6 ounces
283 grams	10 ounces
397 grams	14 ounces
454 grams	16 ounces
907 grams	32 ounces

LENGTH

IMPERIAL	METRIC
1 inch	2.54 centimeters
2 inches	5 centimeters
4 inches	10 centimeters
6 inches	15 centimeters
8 inches	20 centimeters
10 inches	25 centimeters
12 inches	30 centimeters

INDEX

About the Authors

Tracey West had a blast in the late nineties and the zeroes writing tie-in books for *The Powerpuff Girls*, *Pokémon*, *Samurai Jack*, *Ben 10*, and other animated series. Today she is best known for writing the bestselling Dragon Masters books.

Lisa Kingsley has more than 30 years' experience as a food writer, editor, and recipe developer. She collaborated on *Disney: Cooking with Magic: A Century of Recipes* (Insight Editions, 2023) and *Smithsonian American Table: The Foods, People, and Innovations that Feed Us* (Harvest, 2023).

Author Acknowledgments

Tracey would like to thank Anna Wostenberg and Insight Editions for bringing her back into the candy-colored world of *The Powerpuff Girls*; and most importantly, her mom and dad, who let her watch cartoons every Saturday morning when she was a kid.

INSIGHT
EDITIONS

PO Box 3088
San Rafael, CA 94912
www.insighteditions.com

Find us on Facebook: www.facebook.com/InsightEditions
Follow us on Instagram: @insighteditions

ISBN: 979-8-88663-576-8

Publisher: Raoul Goff
SVP, Group Publisher: Vanessa Lopez
VP, Creative: Chrissy Kwasnik
VP, Manufacturing: Alix Nicholaeff
Art Director: Stuart Smith
Senior Designer: Judy Wiatrek Trum
Senior Editor: Anna Wostenberg
Editorial Assistant: Sami Alvarado
VP, Senior Executive Project Editor: Vicki Jaeger
Production Manager: Deena Hashem
Senior Production Manager, Subsidiary Rights: Lina s Palma-Temena

Recipes by Lisa Kingsley
Written by Tracey West
Photography by Waterbury Publications, Inc.

Insight Editions, in association with Roots of Peace, will plant two trees for each tree used in the
manufacturing of this book. Roots of Peace is an internationally renowned humanitarian organization
dedicated to eradicating land mines worldwide and converting war-torn lands into productive farms
and wildlife habitats. Roots of Peace will plant two million fruit and nut trees in Afghanistan and
provide farmers there with the skills and support necessary for sustainable land use.

Manufactured in China by Insight Editions

10 9 8 7 6 5 4 3 2 1